STUPID SPORTS

STUPID SPORTS

Leland Gregory

**Andrews McMeel
Publishing®**

a division of Andrews McMeel Universal

Andrews McMeel Publishing
a division of Andrews McMeel Universal
1130 Walnut Street, Kansas City, Missouri 64106

www.andrewsmcmeel.com

15 16 17 18 19 RR4 10 9 8 7 6 5 4 3 2

ISBN: 978-1-4494-2735-1

Library of Congress Control Number: 2012955064

ATTENTION: SCHOOLS AND BUSINESSES
Andrews McMeel books are available at quantity discounts with bulk purchase for educational, business, or sales promotional use. For information, please e-mail the Andrews McMeel Publishing Special Sales Department: specialsales@amuniversal.com.

STUPID SPORTS

TWO'S COMPANY

April 17, 1993—the Baltimore Orioles versus the California Angels. It was a play that had all the makings of a grand slam. The bases were loaded, and the Orioles only had one man out. Mike Devereaux stepped up to the plate and cracked the ball as hard as he could. The second the leather hit the wood, the runner at third, Jeff Tackett, headed for home. But Devereaux's line drive didn't make it to the wall and was caught by the Angel's center fielder. Tackett shook his head and trotted back to third base. But when he got there, he noticed his teammate, Brady Anderson, the runner from second, was standing on third. And standing next to Anderson was Chito Martinez—the runner from first. The Angels' catcher, John Orton, tagged all three, and two were called out for a double play that ended the inning. *Sports Illustrated* called it the stupidest play of the year. "It wouldn't have been the stupidest play until Chito arrived at third," said the Angels' third baseman. "I think he thought there was a fight, so he ran across the field to get in it." Remember, folks: The players who hang out together get called out together.

"I'd rather win two or three, lose one, win two or three more. I'm a great believer in things evening out. If you win a whole bunch in a row, somewhere along the line you're going to lose some, too."

—Los Angeles Dodgers manager Walt "Smokey" Alston,
Los Angeles Times, May 7, 1976

THE FINAL SHOT

In 1974, NBA scoring star "Pistol Pete" Maravich told reporter Andy Nuzzo of the *Beaver County (Pennsylvania) Times*, "I don't want to play 10 years [in the NBA] and then die of a heart attack when I'm 40." Maravich played an impressive 10 years in the league and retired in 1980. Eight years later, on January 5, 1988, Maravich was playing a pickup game at the First Church of the Nazarene in Pasadena, California, when he suffered a major heart attack and died—he was 40 years old. An autopsy revealed that Maravich suffered from an undiagnosed congenital heart defect that could have ended his career and his life at any time. His last words before collapsing were, "I feel great."

"Teen golfers charged with giving their teammate a wedgie."

—*USA Today* headline, March 28, 2007

A LONG LEAP

Competing in the 1924 Winter Olympics held in Chamonix, France, Norwegian-American ski jumper Anders Haugen barely missed a medal and finished a close fourth. For Haugen, February 1, 1924, was a day he'd never forget, and so was September 12, 1974. What's so special about that date? That's when history was changed. You see, Norwegian sports historian Jakob Vaage had gone over the results of the 1924 Games and noticed a scoring error—Haugen had actually qualified to win bronze. So on September 12, 1974, eighty-five-year-old Haugen came to Norway to accept his long overdue Bronze medal.

NOT QUITE PAR FOR THE COURSE

January 6, 1968, is a day that will live in infamy for English pro golfer Brian Barnes. On the par-4 eighth hole in the French Open Golf Tournament, his ball lay an easy three feet from the cup, and a confident Barnes took aim and fired. But his aim was off, and the ball glanced off the edge. Needless to say, he was a little perturbed. To show his frustration, he backhanded the ball—it missed the hole again and he missed the bogey. It seemed as if Barnes's ball was repelled by the cup, and he batted it back and forth a dozen times, sometimes while the ball was still moving. Finally, he sank the ball, but chalking up the strokes and penalties, he wound up with 11-over-par and a historical record—the most putts ever taken on a single hole in a pro tournament.

Two men filed a lawsuit against the stadium's concession stand at a Philadelphia Phillies baseball game claiming the bartender failed to fill their cups of beer to the rim.

—*Ocala Star-Banner*, May 8, 1998

A SWING AND A MISS

On October 19, 2011, during Game 1 of the World Series between the American League champion Texas Rangers and the National League champion St. Louis Cardinals, play-by-play announcer Joe Buck mentioned that Cardinals relief pitcher Marc Rzepczynski's nickname was "Scrabble" because of his letter-intensive last name. Fellow broadcaster Tim McCarver chimed in by saying, "It's a five-letter word: S-T-R-I-K-E."

FORMER OLYMPIC GYMNAST PAUL HAMM WAS ARRESTED FOR KICKING AND PUNCHING A TAXI DRIVER AND DAMAGING THE CAB WINDOW AFTER REFUSING TO PAY A $23 FARE FOR HIS RIDE HOME.

—The Associated Press, September 8, 2011

CHECK, PLEASE!

Dave Forbes, a Boston Bruins defenseman, has the distinction of being the first NHL player ever charged with criminal assault for actions during a game. Forbes butt-ended Henry Boucha of the Minnesota North Stars in a January 4, 1975, game, fracturing Boucha's cheekbone and opening a gash over his eye, which required thirty stitches. Boucha suffered blurred vision from the incident and never fully recovered. Forbes was arrested and charged with aggravated assault, facing up to five years in prison and a $5,000 fine. However, the nine-day trial ended with a hung jury, and the prosecution chose not to pursue a second jury hearing of the case. So the charges against Forbes were dropped.

The Phillies have been located in Philadelphia since 1883, but from 1883 to 1889, they were called the Philadelphia Quakers. For a short time, 1943 through 1948, they were the Philadelphia Bluejays.

A LONG MAT NAP

Boxers may not be the brightest athletes out there (especially if they suffer from dementia pugilistica, or punch-drunk syndrome), but not using his head cost Jack Dempsey a controversial and still contested fight with Gene Tunney on September 22, 1927, in Chicago. Dempsey clocked Tunney, who dropped like a sack of flour. Referee Dave Barry wouldn't begin the count until Dempsey had retreated because a newly enacted rule mandated that when a fighter knocked down an opponent, he had to immediately go to a neutral corner. But Dempsey wouldn't move. Finally, Barry had to escort The Manassa Mauler to a corner and then go back and begin the count. This gave Tunney a full fourteen seconds on the mat to regain his composure. Once he was back on his feet, he was able to win the fight by points and retain his title. The fight has since become known as the Battle of the Long Count.

. . . .

"I've never seen a team win a pennant without players."
—Cincinnati Reds manager Sparky Anderson,
Los Angeles Times, August 8, 1974

. . . .

NO, I SAID, "HI, JACK!"

Leonard George "Len" Koenecke finally made it to the big leagues after a lifetime filled with dreams and determination. He signed with the New York Giants in 1931, and three years later was traded to the Brooklyn Dodgers. He was a part-time starting outfielder, batting .320 for the year. The next year he was hitting .283 when the Dodgers simply released him in the middle of a road trip, blaming his decline on excessive drinking. Utterly devastated, Koenecke caught a plane to New York, and after drinking a quart of whiskey, he was removed from the plane unconscious. When he regained his composure, he boarded a flight to Buffalo, New York, on September 17, 1935. For reasons unknown, Koenecke attempted to skyjack the plane when it was over Canada. He burst into the cockpit and struggled for control of the plane until the pilot clubbed him over the head with a fire extinguisher. By the time the plane was forced to make an emergency landing on a racetrack, Koenecke had already died of a cerebral hemorrhage.

JOSE CAN YOU SEE?

Within the first few minutes of her rendition of the national anthem at Super Bowl XLV in 2010, Christina Aguilera hit another high note in her career. While Pittsburgh Steelers and Green Bay Packers fans stood in respect and millions of people watched at home, Aguilera sang, "What so proudly we watched at the twilight's last reaming," instead of, "O'er the ramparts we watched, were so gallantly streaming."

"Gators to Face Seminoles with Peters Out"

—Headline from the *Tallahassee Bugle*

RULES IS THE RULES

On September 23, 1845, New York's Knickerbocker Base Ball
Club adopted the first rules governing the play of the modern
game of baseball formulated by bookseller Alexander Cartwright.
One of the new rules included playing with four bases, not the
five that had been in use. Also, the infield would be in the shape
of a diamond instead of oblong. And they graciously disallowed
recording an out by fielding a ball and hitting the batter or
runner anywhere on his body. The new rules worked wonderfully
for everyone except the Knickerbocker Club, which lost on June
19, 1846, to the New York Baseball Club 23–1.

· ·

**The Eighty-third United States Congress officially
declared Alexander Cartwright the inventor of the
modern game of baseball on June 3, 1953.**

· ·

A ROSE BY ANY OTHER NAME

With a name like the Chicago White Stockings you might think the team would eventually become the White Sox. But the White Stockings (1870–1889) was actually the original name of the Chicago Cubs. Then they became the Chicago Colts (1890–1897) and later the Chicago Orphans (1898–1901) before becoming the Cubs in 1902.

Acting on a Major League Baseball policy that permitted fans to wave only "baseball-related" banners, officials confiscated the Reverend Guy Aubrey's "John 3:16" banner in 1990. In 1993, the preacher returned with another banner that proclaimed, "Go Reds—John 3:16."

—Press release, The Rutherford Institute, June 17, 1997

CUE YOU, TOO!

It's sometimes referred to as the match between "The Fox and the Fly." On September 7, 1865, billiards player Louis Fox was having a remarkable run against challenger John Deery at the Rochester, New York, World Billiards Championships. To his chagrin, a fly continued to pester Fox, and eventually it landed on his cue ball. Fox impatiently brushed the fly away with the tip of his cue and inadvertently tapped the cue ball, ending his run. Deery unleashed a run of 165 points, and Fox was unable to get another shot. Later, a distraught Fox threw himself into a nearby river and drowned.

• •

In November 1998, fifty-eight-year-old Japanese billiards player Junuske Inoue was suspended for two years from competing after he tested positive for a muscle-building hormone.

• •

GIVING THEM
THE BIRD

The Atlanta Falcons proudly took the field for the first time
on September 11, 1966, as the NFL's newest expansion team.
This was a big deal for the city of Atlanta, and it needed to
be a spectacular launch. A sellout crowd was on hand with a
distinguished lineup of politicians and dignitaries. The crowd
eagerly watched the sky as a live falcon was released. It had been
trained to swoop over the crowd and then land majestically on its
perch to watch over its namesake team. The fifty-four thousand
fans gaped in awe as the graceful bird of prey winged out over
the field and kept flying—never to be seen again. The stadium
was prepared for just such a situation, and there was another
falcon on hand to fill in. Unfortunately, the second one did the
same thing, as did the third. After watching the team lose its
first nine games in a row, a dismal start to the inaugural season,
fans soon understood why the falcons were embarrassed to be
associated with the Falcons.

"If I'm out somewhere and
a player comes in, I don't want him
to turn around and walk
out just because I'm there.
I expect him to say hello, have
a drink—and then get out."

—Three-time Major League Baseball manager Hank Bauer,
Sports Illustrated, September 11, 1964

NO STOMACH FOR THE GAME

Both teams were in their stance and the ball was ready to be snapped. The quarterback was calling out the signals. Denver Bronco defensive tackle Darren Drozdov was in his position opposite the offensive center. During the tense few milliseconds before the ball went into play in this August 1993 exhibition game, Drozdov suddenly made a messy defensive foul—he vomited on the ball. After the game, Drozdov told reporters for the *Baltimore Sun* (August 29, 1993), "I get sick a lot. I was a quarterback in high school, and I'd start throwing up on my center's back. I don't have a lot of control out there." Well, at least his heart was in the right place.

"*Just remember,
if you ream me,
I got the last ream.*"

—Three-time Major League Baseball manager Hank Bauer,
Sports Illustrated, September 11, 1964

DEAF AS A POST BUT SMART AS A FOX

The Norfolk Blues were a team of collegiate all-stars considered by many, including themselves, to be the final word in college football. So when they went up against Gallaudet, the Blues thought it was a sure win—Gallaudet was a school for the hearing impaired. Norfolk's egos were bigger than their helmets, and they decided that since their opponents were deaf, they wouldn't even bother calling out signals or getting into a huddle. This classic blunder in 1912 ended in a shutout, 20–0, and the winners weren't the Norfolk Blues—they were the hearing-impaired Gallaudet athletes. How? Although Gallaudet team members were deaf, they could still read lips, and they understood every play Norfolk was going to make. I'm sure that after the game Norfolk's fans gave their team a few signs anyone could understand.

"It's a humbling thing being humble."

—Former Ohio State running back Maurice Clarett, on his chances of being a first-round pick in the 2005 NFL draft. He was selected by the Broncos in the third round, but they eventually released him.

GOOD OLD-FASHIONED NAMES

Baseball teams from the Federal League (1914–1915)

BALTIMORE TERRAPINS

BROOKLYN TIP-TOPS

NEWARK PEPPERS

PITTSBURGH REBELS

ST. LOUIS TERRIERS

Upon hearing Joe Jacoby of the Washington Redskins say, "I'd run over my own mother to win the Super Bowl," Matt Millen of the Raiders said: "To win, I'd run over Joe's mom, too."

A WHALE OF A SWIMMER

On two different occasions, long-distance open-water swimmer Lynne Cox has held the record for fastest swimmer to cross the English Channel: in 1972, nine hours and fifty-seven minutes; in 1973, nine hours and thirty-six minutes. In 1975, she broke the gender barrier as the first woman to swim the fourteen-mile Cook Strait in New Zealand. The next year, she became the first person to swim the Strait of Magellan in Chile, and the first to swim around the Cape of Good Hope in South Africa.

On August 7, 1987, she swam across the Bering Strait from Alaska's Little Diomede Island to Big Diomede Island in the Soviet Union. She traveled the 2.7-mile distance in two hours, enduring the 44-degree temperature wearing only a bathing suit and a cap. Cox attributed her accomplishment and her survival to her five-foot, six-inch, 209-pound frame. It was reasoned that like a seal, her 40 percent fat content insulated her body from the cold.

· ·

In the tenth inning of the seventh game of the 1991 World Series, Atlanta Braves owner Ted Turner fell asleep.

· ·

BLOWIN'
IN THE WIND

On May 27, 1981, outfielder Amos Otis was up to bat for Kansas City. His swing didn't fully connect with the ball, and he sent a worm burner along the third baseline. The ball quickly lost momentum and began slowly rolling right down the foul line. So Seattle third baseman Lenny Randle had a brainstorm—he dropped down on all fours and blew on the ball with all his might so it would cross the foul line. It was a cute idea, but the home-plate umpire ruled that Randle's attempt was full of hot air, and he awarded Otis first base on a hit. Randle seemed to have been bitten by the laughter bug after this blowhard antic—after leaving baseball, he became a stand-up comic.

"Slow thinkers are part of the game too. Some of these slow thinkers can hit a ball a long way."

—Cleveland Indians manager Alvin "Blackie" Dark
Baseball Digest, January 1968

URINE TROUBLE NOW

According to an August 12, 2011, article in the *New York Post*, eighteen-year-old US Ski Team member Robert "Sandy" Vietze was dismissed from the developmental squad and lost his chance to compete in the 2014 Winter Games in Russia. Was he a piss-poor performer? Nope, he was a piss-poor passenger aboard a JetBlue airliner when he drunkenly urinated on a sleeping eleven-year-old girl. The incident quickly leaked out when the girl's father and his other daughter, who were returning from the restrooms, caught Vietze midstream. "I was drunk, and I did not realize I was pissing on her leg," the six-foot-four, 195-pound Vietze later told police after admitting he had consumed eight alcoholic beverages before boarding the flight.

. . . .

Basketball great Charles Barkley of the Phoenix Suns claimed that he was misquoted in a book about his life and career. The book was his autobiography.

. . . .

GOODBYE, MR. SPALDING!

It's a name that will be forever associated with baseball. Am I talking about Ty Cobb, Lou Gehrig, Babe Ruth? Nope, I'm talking about Albert Goodwill Spalding. In addition to manufacturing baseballs and other sporting equipment, Spalding was a famous pitcher for the Boston Red Stockings. From 1871 through the 1875 season, he reigned as baseball's best pitcher. But that wasn't good enough, so on February 3, 1876, he and his brother J. Walter pooled together $800 in savings and began a sporting-goods company, A.G. Spalding and Brothers, which is now the oldest company of its kind. A.G. Spalding was first in several sports; it manufactured the first official National League baseball, the first American basketball (created for the inventor of the game, Dr. James Naismith), the first American tennis ball, the first football, and the first golf ball. With all this business success, did Spalding give up the game he loved? No. In 1876, playing for Chicago in the National League, he won forty-seven games and lost just thirteen, with a 1.75 ERA and pitching the ball bearing his name.

TOM STAFFORD OF MISSION VIEJO, CALIFORNIA, SLICED A GOLF BALL TOO HARD TO THE LEFT, CAUSING IT TO RICOCHET OFF A STEEL POLE AND CRACK HIM IN THE FOREHEAD. HE SUED THE GOLF COURSE FOR DAMAGES AND WON AN $8,500 SETTLEMENT IN NOVEMBER 1993.

NOTHING TO LOVE

If you thought John McEnroe was the most foul-mouthed bad boy of tennis, you ain't heard nothing yet. In a 1992 local tournament, Zambian tennis player Musumba Bwayla beat Lighton Ndefwayl, and Ndefwayl had this to say: "Musumba Bwayla is a stupid man and a hopeless player. He has a huge nose and is cross-eyed. Girls hate him. He beat me because my jockstrap was too tight and because when he serves he farts, and that made me lose my concentration, for which I am famous throughout Zambia." Don't you just love a good sport?

—*The Observer*, October 3, 2004

· ·

Fred Lorz finished first in the marathon in the Summer Olympics of 1904. Just before he was handed the gold medal, it was discovered that he rode in a car for eleven miles of the race.

· ·

A POOR EXCUSE FOR A PLAYER

Players have come up with all kinds of excuses about why they were unable to play in a particular game. But New York Rangers goalie Gilles Gratton requested a deferment because of an injury he sustained in combat. On February 11, 1977, Gratton told Rangers coach John Ferguson that he couldn't participate in the day's game because of a leg injury, and Ferguson questioned the goalie because he didn't remember Gratton being injured in a previous game. Gratton, nicknamed "Gratoony the Loony," was a firm believer in reincarnation, and he explained that the injury was sustained when he was a soldier in the Franco-Prussian War in 1870.

The Pittsburgh Pirates have been in the same place since the 1880s. However, the original name of the team was the Allegheny Innocents (1882–1886), and from 1887 to 1889 they were the Pittsburgh Alleghenys. In 1890, they were known as the Pittsburgh Innocents, and since 1891 they've been the Pirates.

A CONGRESSIONAL PARDON

From 1901 to 1971, the District of Columbia had two major league teams. The first was known as the Senators, until 1961, when they were renamed the Nationals, and they eventually became the Minnesota Twins. The other team was also called the Senators, from 1961 to 1971, when they became the Texas Rangers. Are you still with me? When Washington, D.C., got another team in 2005, the choice for a name was once again between the Washington Nationals or the Washington Senators. So why did the Nationals win out? Because Mayor Anthony Williams wanted to make a statement about the district's lack of representation in Congress. It would be an outrage, he claimed, to have the team named the Senators because Washington doesn't have any senators.

ONE OF THE MOST ONE-SIDED
WOMEN'S COLLEGE BASKETBALL
GAMES IN HISTORY OCCURRED
ON JANUARY 10, 1931, WHEN
MAGNOLIA A&M SLAUGHTERED
JONESBORO BAPTIST 143–1.

MISSED IT BY
THAT MUCH

The Poly, or more formally, the Polytechnic Marathon, was an
annual event from 1909 to 1996, and it was organized by the
Polytechnic Harriers, the athletics club of the Polytechnic at
Regent Street in London. Even though the marathon was well
established, things got a little turned around during the May 18,
1912, race. As the twenty-three runners entered the stadium,
they were accidentally told to go the wrong way around, thereby
only running 480 yards instead of the 840 yards needed to
officially finish the marathon. James Corkery of Canada was
declared the winner, and he thought he had achieved a world
record. He was later informed that his time of 2 hours, 36
minutes, and 55 seconds could not be recognized because it was
short of the full marathon distance.

ON JANUARY 25, 1924, THE FIRST
WINTER OLYMPICS BEGAN IN CHAMONIX,
FRANCE. THESE INITIAL WINTER
GAMES HAD SIXTEEN COUNTRIES
REPRESENTED, AND ONLY A TOTAL
OF ELEVEN FEMALE COMPETITORS.

ALL TOGETHER NOW

In 1949, Pittsburgh pitcher Bill "Bugs" Werle tossed one across the plate, and Phillies right fielder Bill Nicholson hit a high pop-up that was on a trajectory to land somewhere near the mound. It was an easy out, and Werle simply called for one of his fielders to step in by yelling, "Eddie's got it! Eddie's got it!" Catcher Eddie Fitzgerald, first baseman Eddie Stevens, third baseman Eddie Bockman, Werle himself, and everyone in the stands watched in amazement as the ball fell untouched to the ground.

ON APRIL 27, 1908, THE FOURTH
SUMMER OLYMPIC GAMES OF THE
MODERN ERA OPENED IN LONDON.
FOR THE FIRST TIME IN OLYMPICS
HISTORY, THERE WERE MORE WOMEN
COMPETITORS (THIRTY-SEVEN) THAN
NATIONS COMPETING (TWENTY-TWO).

THAT'S USING YOUR HEAD

Ben Crenshaw was on the eighteenth hole at the PGA championship on August 9, 1986, and his ball barely skirted the cup. Gentle Ben flipped his iron into the air in frustration and, in this case, failed to keep his eye on the club. It bonked him on the head, opening up a gash. Blurry eyed, Ben two putted to complete the round and was then carted off to the hospital, where he required three stitches.

. . . .

The world's first recorded international tennis match occurred on January 31, 1505, between Philip, Archduke of Austria and King of Castille, and the Marquis of Dorset. Archduke Philip even graciously agreed to spot the Marquis a 15–0 lead in each game. Did Philip have something up his sleeve? No, he had something in his hand—a *battoir* (racket). The marquis, on the other hand, still played with his *paume*, the palm of his hand.

. . . .

NICE WHILE IT LASTED

In the final event of the Moscow Olympic pentathlon competition on July 24, 1980, an exhausted Olga Rukavishnikova of the U.S.S.R. took second place in the eight-hundred-meter run. Her combined total points in the five-event pentathlon gave her an all-time world mark, but she didn't have time to celebrate her accomplishment. Four-tenths of a second later, fellow countrywoman Nadyezhda Tkachenko crossed the finish line in third place, garnering enough points to give her the world record over Rukavishnikova. Even though she was bumped from that world record, Rukavishnikova set a new one for the shortest time that anyone had ever held a world record.

"I walk into our clubhouse,
and it's like walking into the Mayo
Clinic. We have four doctors,
three therapists and five trainers.
Back when I broke in, we had
one trainer, who carried a bottle
of rubbing alcohol—and by the
seventh inning he had drunk it all."

—Los Angeles Dodgers manager Tommy Lasorda,
Sports Illustrated, May 29, 1989

WITH ONLY TWO LAPS REMAINING DURING THE 1912 INDIANAPOLIS 500, RALPH DEPALMA'S MERCEDES CAME TO A HALT AFTER A PISTON CRACKED. NOT ONE TO GIVE UP EASILY, DEPALMA LEAPED OUT OF HIS IMMOBILE MOBILE AND, ALONG WITH HIS MECHANIC, BEGAN PUSHING IT TOWARD THE FINISH LINE. SO WHY DID DEPALMA PUT IN SO MUCH EFFORT JUST TO FINISH IN ELEVENTH PLACE? BECAUSE AT THAT TIME, A DRIVER COULD ONLY QUALIFY FOR PRIZE MONEY IF THEY COMPLETED THE ENTIRE TWO HUNDRED LAPS.

FLOAT LIKE A BUTTERFLY, THINK LIKE A BEE

He may have been the greatest, but Muhammad Ali certainly wasn't the brightest. In fact, he was saved from the draft in the U.S. Armed Forces in 1964 because his reading and writing skills were below normal. But on February 17, 1966, the Selective Service lowered the minimum acceptable grade from thirty to fifteen, thus making Ali's sixteen a passing score and qualifying him for the draft. The army reclassified the heavyweight champ from 1Y ("Registrant available for military service, but qualified only in case of war or national emergency") to 1A ("Available for unrestricted military service"). It was then that Ali refused to serve and was eventually stripped of his title.

· ·

At Ali's trial on June 20, 1967, the jury deliberated a short twenty-one minutes before finding him guilty. The Court of Appeals upheld the conviction, and the case went to the Supreme Court. On June 28, 1971, in *Clay v. United States*, the Supreme Court unanimously reversed his conviction for refusing induction.

· ·

47

NAME-CHANGING GAME CHANGERS

The Los Angeles Dodgers started as the Brooklyn Atlantics (1883–1884) before becoming the Brooklyn Grays (1885–1887), Brooklyn Grooms (1888–1895), Brooklyn Bridegrooms (1896–1898), Brooklyn Superbas (1899–1910), Brooklyn Trolley Dodgers (1911–1912), Brooklyn Dodgers (1913), Brooklyn Robins (1914–1931), and Brooklyn Dodgers again (1932–1957), until finally becoming the Los Angeles Dodgers in 1958.

"**The greatest feeling in the world is to win a major league game. The second-greatest feeling is to lose a major league game.**"

—Pittsburgh Pirates manager Chuck Tanner,
Sporting News, July 15, 1985

I'M KEEPING MY EYE ON YOU

Charles Wayne Brown of Newton, Iowa, was hit in the right eye by an errant golf ball stroked by car salesman Bill Samuelson in 1982. Brown's eye suffered permanent damage, and he sued Samuelson for failing to yell "fore" before he hit the ball. The lawsuit was dismissed in 1984.

. . . .

At the 1959 Memphis Open Invitational, pro golfer Tommy Bolt was assessed what some have called the stinkiest fine in PGA tour history. Bolt was penalized $250 for unsportsmanlike behavior after he loudly farted just as his opponent was about to putt.

. . . .

GRID IRON FISTED LAW

"It shall be unlawful for any visiting football team or player to carry, convey, tote, kick, throw, pass, or otherwise transport or propel any inflated pigskin across the University of Arizona goal line or score a safety within the confines of the City of Tucson, County of Pima, State of Arizona."

—Tucson, Arizona, statute. Violators can be fined $300 and sentenced to not less than three months in the city jail.

A QUACK IN THE ICE

Wild Wing is the name of the mascot for the Anaheim Ducks of the National Hockey League. It was chosen in a Name the Mascot write-in contest. During the season opener in 1995, Wild Wing attempted to trampoline over a wall of fire, but he just couldn't wing it. He landed on the wall and caught on fire. Fortunately, the Ducks cheerleaders were there to extinguish him before he became extra crispy. Wild Wing is also noted for being the first mascot to descend onto the ice from the rafters of the arena (again in 1995), but the wire stopped short, leaving the duck dangling fifty feet above the ice.

· ·

In a 2003 game in Calgary, Edmonton Oilers coach Craig MacTavish became so infuriated by the annoying antics of the Calgary Flames' mascot, Harvey the Hound, that he ripped out Harvey's furry red tongue and tossed it to the crowd.

· ·

HE AIN'T GOT THE BALLS!

Robert Carnathan was charged with beating a seventy-nine-year-old man to death in a conflict over collecting lost golf balls on a golf course in Quincy, Massachusetts. Carnathan routinely collected balls at the course and sold them back for a discount, and he didn't want the other man barging in on his turf. According to a November 13, 2002, article in the *Boston Herald*, the victim had only wanted a single golf ball to give to his grandson.

· ·

In 1977, Harvey Gartley of Saginaw, Michigan, was set to fight Dennis Culette in a Golden Gloves boxing competition. Only forty-seven seconds after the opening bell, Gartley was counted out by a knockout, but Culette never laid a glove on him. The young Gartley was so excited during the match that he danced himself into exhaustion and fell to the canvas—knocking himself out and losing the fight.

· ·

IT'S A MIRACLE!

Legendary coach Knute Rockne and his Notre Dame team
were up against Georgia Tech, a team with the potential to
give his Fighting Irish a black eye. Rockne had a reputation for
encouraging and firing up his team (remember, "Win one for the
Gipper"?), but the week before the Georgia Tech game, he was at
a loss on how to prime their pump. However, just before kickoff,
Knute produced an authentic telegram addressed to him from
his sick son, and he read it to the team. With tears in his eyes,
Knute announced, "Here's a telegram from my sick little boy, Bill,
who's critically ill in the hospital. It says: 'I want Daddy's team to
win.'" Hearts swelled, tears were stifled, and fierce determination
grew in the minds and bodies of his team. The Irish dominated
the game and crushed Georgia Tech 13–3. Later, when the team
arrived back home, whom should they see leading the cheering
and welcoming crowd at the train station? Knute's son Bill,
looking healthy as a horse. It turned out that Knute had written
the telegraph and had it sent to himself before the game.

WHAT GOES DOWN MUST COME UP

In an attempt to catch a baseball from the highest distance ever, a blimp hovering eight-hundred feet above the ground dropped five baseballs for former American League catcher Joe Sprinz to glove. The spectacle took place at San Francisco's Treasure Island on July 3, 1939. The crowd watched in amazement as Sprinz, who missed the first four balls, was able to successfully mitt the fifth. Unfortunately, he did not take into account Newton's third law of motion—every action has an equal and opposite reaction. The ball slammed so hard into Sprinz's glove that it snapped back, hitting him in the face and loosening five of his teeth.

"No, we don't cheat. And even if we did, I'd never tell you."

—Los Angeles Dodgers manager Tommy Lasorda,
Parade, January 1, 1989

OUR HATS ARE
OFF TO HIM

"It means more than just a hat. It's like my crown. It's like asking
a king to remove his crown."

— Twenty-two-year-old Charles Littleton, angrily refusing to remove
his Los Angeles Dodgers baseball cap during a Saginaw City Council
meeting. According to a November 13, 2006, report on Flint, Michigan's
WJRT-TV, Littleton became defiant after he was asked to either
remove his hat or leave, and he was eventually tasered by police.

• •

**"You can have money piled to the ceiling, but the size of
your funeral is still going to depend on the weather."**

— Pittsburgh Pirates manager Chuck Tanner,
Sporting News, May 20, 1979

• •

THE COLOR BARRIER GRAND SLAM

They were called the Dolly Vardens, and in 1867 they were the first professional baseball team to actually pay their players. What makes this team even more historic isn't just the fact that all the players were African American, but that they were all African American women. Two years later, the first men's professional baseball team, the Cincinnati Red Stockings, finally began paying the players.

. . . .

The Louisville Colonels only supplied three baseballs for their game with the Brooklyn Grooms (later the Brooklyn Dodgers) on May 23, 1895. At that time, it was customary for fans to throw the balls back from the stands, but by the third inning, all three were unusable. Someone was dispatched to get more balls, but the streetcar he rode broke down. Brooklyn was awarded the victory since the rules stated that the home team was responsible for making sure there were enough balls.

. . . .

A FLAGRANT FOUL

The coach of a youth basketball team playing in Fayetteville, Georgia, became more and more argumentative because of referee Oliver Lewis Wood's bad calls. After the game, as reported in the February 14, 2001, edition of the *Atlanta Journal-Constitution*, the referee had had enough of the backbiting comments from the coach of the seven- and eight-year-old players, so the ref took out a knife and stabbed him. The coach, whose day job was county marshal, needed seventeen stitches, and the referee, by day a Baptist minister, was arrested. And they wonder why kids don't have any role models these days!

Originally, the St. Louis Cardinals were the St. Louis Brown Stockings or the Browns (1882–1898). They changed their name to the Perfectos in 1899, and became the Cardinals in 1900.

THE NAME'S THE THING

Baseball Teams from the International League (1884–Present)

1894, ALLENTOWN BINGOES

1962–1965, ATLANTA CRACKERS

1886–1887, BINGHAMTON CRICKETS

1901, BROCKTON B'S

1886–PRESENT, BUFFALO BISONS

1971–1983, CHARLESTON CHARLIES

1889–1890, DETROIT WOLVERINES

1892, ELMIRA GLADIATORS

"It's déjà vu all over again."

—Yogi Berra, in the early 1960s, afte
witnessing Mickey Mantle and Roger Maris h
several back-to-back home runs for the Yankees

OH, BROTHER

Most people have heard of the legendary Jesse Owens, who gained international fame for beating Germany (and Hitler) at the 1936 Olympics in Berlin. His feat overshadowed nearly everything about that particular Olympics—even the name of the man whom he beat in the 200-meter dash by four-tenths of a second, Mack Robinson, another African-American sprinter. But a decade later, the name Robinson redefined sports and the color barrier when Mack's younger brother, Jackie Robinson, debuted with the Brooklyn Dodgers.

· ·

In July 1979, Wallace Williams of the Virgin Islands ran such a slow pace in the marathon of the Eighth Pan American Games in San Juan, Puerto Rico, that by the time he reached the stadium, it was closed and everyone had gone home.

· ·

WATCH YOUR LANGUAGE

During a World Cup soccer competition in 1994, Addison, Texas, city officials warned restaurant owners to be wary of possible credit card fraud perpetrated by Nigerians who came to support their soccer team. Councilman Dick Wilke said restaurant owners should inform the police "if thirty people come in speaking Nigerian." There's only one problem with this measure of alertness. There is no such language as Nigerian—the country's official language is English.

· ·

During the 1989 Tour de France, reigning champion Pedro Delgado of Spain finished third—he started almost three minutes late because he was busy signing autographs.

· ·

HIGH-TECH BLOWOUT

Cleveland Browns coach Paul Brown was always on the cutting edge of innovation. Brown was the first coach to use game films to teach his players about their opponents, and the first to hire a staff of full-time assistants. He created the modern face mask and developed what was called the "taxi squad," a clever way of circumventing the All-America Football Conference's thirty-three-man limit by keeping an additional group of players who were off the roster and were paid by Browns owner Mickey McBride's taxi company. So on October 14, 1956, when he was exploring the latest technological advancement to help his team, Brown equipped his quarterback with a special helmet fitted with a radio receiver. The idea was that he could then call in the plays from the sidelines. But there was one problem: The Browns' opponents, the New York Giants, quickly figured out what was going on, and it was a simple matter for them to tune into the same frequency and hear all the plays. The Browns had no idea the Giants had outsmarted them, and by the time it became clear what was going on, it was too late. The Giants beat the technologically savvy Browns, 21–9.

The football team the Cleveland Browns was named after their first coach, Paul Brown. Brown was later instrumental in founding another football team, the Cincinnati Bengals.

THE RAINBOW RODEO

Jen Vrana, president and founder of the Liberty Gay Rodeo Association, is determined to prove that gays and lesbians can be just as macho as straights. In the May 2008 contest held in Devon, Pennsylvania, competitors participated in steer riding, calf roping, and goat dressing. According to a May 13, 2008, Reuters article, goat dressing is a contest during which contestants compete to "put hot-pink underwear on the hind quarters of an uncooperative goat in the shortest time." Vrana defended the goat-dressing contest by saying, "This proves that we are normal. . . . This is an all-American sport, and we are all-American people."

FOOT BRAWL

We've all heard of the British soccer hooligans—rough fans of the sport who wreak havoc before, during, and after a game—but who is really the roughest element of the sport? How about the referees? That's right. A South African soccer referee was charged with murder after he shot dead a player who disagreed with him about a goal. The referee, Lebogang Petrus Mokgethi, claimed he was acting in self-defense because the player, Isaac Mkhwetha, lunged at him with a knife after the opposing team scored a goal. The game was held in the gold-mining town of Hartbeesfontein, 110 miles southwest of Johannesburg. I'll bet it made the halftime festivities pale in comparison.

"When we win, I'm so happy I eat a lot. When we lose, I'm so depressed I eat a lot. When we're rained out, I'm so disappointed I eat a lot."

—Los Angeles Dodgers former manager Tommy Lasorda,
Forbes, Vol. 174, Issue 9, 2004

IF YOU SAY IT, THEY WILL LISTEN

A Pittsburgh Pirates broadcaster broke into coverage of a Giants–Pirates baseball game to report that actor James Earl Jones had died. "A lot of us in baseball have a lot of feelings about *Field of Dreams* and the soliloquy he gave in it," announcer Larry Frattare lamented. A few minutes later, Frattare got back on the microphone with an update on the actor's condition—he was fine; he wasn't dead. The announcer had misunderstood his producer when he tried to tell Frattare that James Earl Ray, convicted murderer of the Reverend Martin Luther King, Jr., had died. "I don't feel glad about it. In fact, I felt like a real fool," Frattare said. James Earl Jones was quite relieved to hear that he wasn't dead.

STRIPPED OFF THE TEAM

A female student at California State, Fullerton was forced by her track coach to either quit the team or quit her part-time job. The student eventually decided to quit the team and not give up her night job as an exotic dancer, since it was the night job that made it possible for her to go to college in the first place. Her coach said allowing her to strip after school "would detract from the image and accomplishments of her teammates, the athletic department, and the university." So how did the coach find out about the girl's profession? Members of the school's baseball team attended the club where she performed and caught her act. Commenting on the coach's criticism of "the image and accomplishments of . . . the university," the stripper explained that although the baseball team members were in the audience wearing school caps and sweaters, in her act she doesn't wear any clothing that identifies her school.

. . . .

"At all those banquets, stars get up and give credit to their coaches and parents. I give credit to no one. I made myself what I am today."

—Bob Uecker, *Baseball Digest*, June 1972

. . . .

WORD UP

With summer approaching, a group of students at the Albany campus of the State University of New York decided to throw a theme picnic and chose to honor Baseball Hall of Famer Jackie Robinson, who broke baseball's color barrier. A gathering of about forty students protested the use of the word "picnic" to promote the event, insisting "picnic" originally was a racist code word that referred to lynching blacks. Actually, any English teacher could have told them that "picnic" came into the English language in about 1748 and was derived from the French word *pique-nique*, which meant the same thing. But that wouldn't have deterred these naysayers. In fact, the school's affirmative-action director released a memo asking everyone to stop using the word, regardless of its origin. "Whether the claims are true or not, the point is the word offended." The group throwing the, uh, event during which you eat food outside on a blanket, changed the phrase to an "outing." But that word didn't sit too well with the campus's gay and lesbian community, and it was removed. So, after everyone had his or her say, the event was promoted without the use of a noun to describe what it was.

JUST DON'T JUMP OVER THE NET

Okay, is it table tennis or Ping-Pong? Well, Ping-Pong was the name for a particularly elaborate version of the game developed by English game maker John Jaques & Son Ltd., of London, which trademarked it in 1901. Other manufacturers were forced to call their versions of the game something else, so they settled on "table tennis." A predecessor to Ping-Pong was a game called Gossima, and there were other names for it, including Whiff-Whaff, Pom-Pom, and Pim-Pam. John Jaques of London eventually sold the American rights to the Ping-Pong name to Parker Brothers.

. . . .

The Chinese dominate the world of table tennis. They have won the Men's World Championship 60 percent of the time since 1959; Chinese women have won all but two of the World Championships since 1971; and at the 2008 Beijing Olympics and 2012 London Olympics, China won all possible gold medals. Surprisingly, the game wasn't introduced in China until 1901.

. . . .

73

A FISHY TRADE

Some baseball pitchers are worth their weight in gold—others, I guess, are only worth their weight in catfish. In one of the most bizarre trades in Western Baseball League history, the Oxnard, California, Pacific Suns swapped minor league pitcher Ken Krahenbuhl to the Greenville, Mississippi, Bluesmen for, among other things, ten pounds of catfish. "I still can't believe they traded me for some catfish," Krahenbuhl said in a July 29, 1998, article in the *Los Angeles Times*. "It's totally ridiculous." But the July 1998 trade turned out to be a good catch for the Bluesmen when Krahenbuhl pitched a perfect game for his new team. "The Suns could have gotten some players in exchange for me to help their ball club, instead of the stinking catfish, but they just don't care," he said. "They traded me for catfish. Can you believe that?"

74

The Krahenbuhl trade is considered to be one of baseball's strangest, but not *the* strangest. In 1997, the Greenville Bluesmen traded an unopened Muddy Waters record and fifty pounds of pheasant to Sioux Falls of the Northern League in exchange for a second baseman.

AND THE RACE IS ON

At 8:55 a.m. on November 28, 1895, four gasoline-powered and two electrically driven "motocycles" took off for a 54-mile loop along the lakeshore from Jackson Park in Chicago, to Evanston, Illinois, and back again in the first-ever American automobile race. The *Chicago Times-Herald* offered $2,000 to the driver finishing first, and J. Frank Duryea won, blazing the 54 miles in 10 hours and 23 minutes. He traveled at an average speed of 5¼ miles per hour, using 3½ gallons of gasoline he'd purchased at a drugstore.

• •

"Persons who are inclined . . . to decry the development of the horseless carriage . . . will be forced . . . to recognize it as an admitted mechanical achievement, highly adapted to some of the most urgent needs of our civilization.

—"The Future of the Motocycle," the *Chicago Times-Herald*, November 29, 1895

• •

BASEBALL ONLY CERBERUS WOULD LOVE

The game of baseball has changed over the years, and I'm not just talking about the designated hitter. How about the triple-header? That's right, a triple-header. On September 1, 1890, for the first and only time in baseball history, teams played three complete nine-inning games in one day. The Brooklyn Grooms faced the Pittsburgh Innocents in a National League triple-header (another positive change is that we don't have too many weird names for baseball teams). The Grooms, the best club in the league, swept all three from the Innocents by scores of 10–9, 3–2, and 8–4. This triple beating pushed the Innocents further away from first place by an unbelievable 66½ games.

THE SWEET SPOT

A high school baseball pitcher in Chicago filed a lawsuit against the makers of Louisville Slugger baseball bats. He claimed the company's aluminum bats were "unreasonably dangerous" to pitchers because they were designed to hit baseballs extremely hard.

. . . .

According to a February 18, 2006, article in the Florence, Alabama, *Times Daily*, a University of North Alabama basketball player was arrested in Town Creek, Alabama, on drug-related charges. The player's name was Reprobatus Bibbs— "reprobate" is defined in the dictionary as "a depraved, unprincipled, or wicked person."

. . . .

BAND ON THE RUN

The band hit a really sour note during the November 1, 1986, football game between Southern Methodist University and Texas A&M. The one-hundred-member Mustang band was out of tune with the officials, who warned the musicians during halftime not to continue playing while the Aggies tried to call plays. But the band decided to turn a deaf ear and kept playing. In the final minutes of the game, A&M was ahead 39–35 and trying to run out the clock, and the band played on. Finally, the game officials had enough and penalized the Mustangs fifteen yards for unsportsmanlike conduct by the band. The call gave the Aggies a first down and gave them plenty of time to run down the clock. You can be pretty sure the Mustangs tried to run down the band members after their loss.

NOT A STOCK ENDING

Stock car driver Danny Elko of Sydney, Australia, was speeding along at 205 miles an hour when he was involved in a five-car pileup. Amazingly, he survived with only a broken leg. He was placed in an ambulance, and it headed for the hospital, but it struck a guardrail traveling at only twenty miles per hour. In a bizarre turn of events, the rear doors of the vehicle opened, tossing the wounded Elko out onto the pavement where he fractured his skull and died.

. . . .

According to a lawsuit filed in Minneapolis, and reported by the *St. Paul Pioneer Press* on June 30, 2006, Minnesota Timberwolves basketball player Eddie Griffin was cited for driving his SUV into a parked car. Police ticketed Griffin only for "inattentive driving," but the cause of his inattentiveness was watching a pornographic video and masturbating while driving drunk.

. . . .

SLEEPER HOLD

High School wrestling isn't always the most entertaining sport to watch, and that was especially true of the match that took place on January 28, 1892, between White Swan High and Highland High, both in the state of Washington. Swan had brought six wrestlers, but Highland had only arrived with five. That shouldn't have been a big problem, but no two of the eleven wrestlers were in the same weight class. Therefore, when it came to recognizing a winner in each match of the head-to-head wrestling meet, one high school or the other was declared the victor on a forfeit score of 6–0. In this nonwrestling wrestling event, White Swan won 36–30 without one second of actual wrestling.

· ·

"Any ballplayer that don't sign autographs for little kids ain't an American. He's a communist."

—Rogers Hornsby, *Saturday Evening Post*,
June 12, 1963

· ·

MARCHING TO A DIFFERENT DRUMMER

They'll never be called wimps and geeks again. During half-time at a 1998 game between Southern University and Prairie View A&M in Beaumont, Texas, the team's marching bands got into an on-field brawl that lasted twenty minutes. No one is sure of the particulars, but it started when the two marching bands passed each other in formation. When it was all over, two $5,000 tubas were bent, and several pieces of uniforms and one saxophone were listed as missing. It was a musical interlude that will live in the hearts and minds of both teams for quite some time. Talk about the battle of the bands!

. . . .

Reuters reported on November 10, 2006, that a Chinese man from the Fujian province had applied to the government to sell female sanitary pads under the trademark of China's star basketball player, Yao Ming.

. . . .

A STROKE OF
BAD LUCK

During the final round of the 1934 U.S. Open, golfer Bobby
Cruickshank was ahead of his competitors by two strokes.
In order to maintain his lead, he had to make the next hole
in four strokes. Cruickshank's drive from the tee was quietly
applauded, and the ball rolled a respectable length down the
fairway. Unfortunately, his follow-up shot was a clinker, and
Cruickshank's hopes sank as he watched his ball sail into the
stream in front of the green and disappear out of sight. But
before his heart could skip a beat, Cruickshank and the amazed
crowd watched as the ball bounced out of the water (probably
ricocheting off a submerged rock) and bounced onto the green,
an unbelievable ten feet from the hole. Cruickshank threw
his club into the air, tipped the brim of his hat, and let out a
yelp of gratitude to the heavens, "Thank you, God!" With his
head exposed and his attention focused on the ball and not
the hurtling club, he smiled broadly at the crowd. The club
changed his expression when it clanked Cruickshank over the
head, knocking him to the ground. He wasn't badly hurt by the
falling 5-iron, but he was unable to regain his composure or his
sure-sightedness, and he wound up third in the competition.
Cruickshank was definitely teed off, but at least the falling club
didn't give him a stroke.

"They've got so many Latin players we're going to have to get a Latin instructor up here."

—Phil Rizzuto, *Sporting News*, April 24, 1989

LEADING THE CHEER

In cheerleading, they use the word "rah." So, what's a rah and where did it come from? Some trace the origin to the word "hurrah," and others believe it was developed in the late 1870s, at Princeton University. The Tigers football team had a male pep squad that supported it from the stands with chants of "Ray, ray, ray! Tiger, tiger, sis, sis, sis! Boom, boom, boom! Aaaah! Princeton, Princeton, Princeton!" On November 2, 1898, student Johnny Campbell became the first cheerleader when football was introduced to the University of Minnesota, where he led the crowd with, "Rah, rah, rah! Ski-u-mah, Hoo-rah! Hoo-rah! Varsity! Varsity! Varsity! Minn-e-so-tah!" to help motivate the Minnesota Gophers. Soon after, the University of Minnesota organized a "yell leader" squad of six male students (the college was all male), who still use Campbell's original cheer.

UPSY-DAISY

There are so many different athletic records they could hardly be contained in one book. But you'll never get a medal for breaking the record skier Chuck Ryan holds. On January 25, 1959, Ryan took off down the sixty-meter slide in the Duluth Invitational when he suddenly realized he had forgotten one important pre-ski detail—he didn't fasten his skis. As he hit the upward curve in the slide, both skis flew off and Ryan sailed into the sky. He came to Earth 148 feet down the landing run in a colossal crash. Ryan wasn't seriously injured in the race, but he holds the record for longest ski jump without skis.

—*Schenectady Gazette*, January 28, 1959

. . . .

**"I set records that will never be equaled. In fact,
I hope 90% of them don't even get printed."**

—Bob Uecker, *Baseball Digest*, June 1972

. . . .

TALK ABOUT HOT PANTS. IN THE 1970S, CRICKETER STAN DAWSON WAS BATTING AT KALGOORLIE, AUSTRALIA, WHEN HE WAS HIT BY THE CRICKET BALL. THE BALL STRUCK HIM IN THE HIP POCKET AND ALTHOUGH THAT MIGHT CREATE A BURNING SENSATION, IT WAS NOTHING COMPARED TO WHAT HAPPENED NEXT—HIS PANTS CAUGHT ON FIRE. APPARENTLY, DAWSON HAD A BOX OF MATCHES IN HIS TROUSERS, AND THE BALL CAUSED THEM TO IGNITE. WHILE HE TRIED TO PUT OUT THE FIRE, HE WAS RUN OUT.

TWO BALLS, NO STRIKES

Baseballs, caps, pennants, and other goodies are all examples of promotional giveaways at baseball parks across the United States. Sometimes it's the giveaways, not the teams, that pull in the big crowds—who can forget the mass appeal of those Beanie Babies? But one Charleston, South Carolina, RiverDogs' free promotion was as warmly received as, well, a free vasectomy, which is exactly what they offered. The minor league RiverDogs withdrew their 1997 Father's Day promotion of a free vasectomy the following day after fans protested. The clip job was nixed by the Roman Catholic Diocese of Charleston, spearheaded by Bishop David Thompson—a season ticket holder, mind you, and a father of a different sort. "We found that clearly people didn't like the idea," said general manager Mark Schuster, adding that the promotion wasn't intended to offend anyone. "We are sensitive to our fans' wants." Makes that Beanie Babies craze seem a little more reasonable, doesn't it?

"I've got a kid six years old. He likes sports, but I definitely won't let him pitch. There would be too many things against him."

—Cleveland Indians pitcher Gaylord Perry,
Los Angeles Herald-Examiner, March 10, 1974

OUT LIKE A FLASH

The skies grew dark during a soccer match in the Democratic Republic of Congo, but the fans kept watching, and the players kept playing. Nothing could dampen the game, they thought, not even a little rain. But attendees at the game got the shock of their lives when lightning crashed down, immediately killing all eleven members of the visiting team. Thirty other people received burns during the weekend match, and "the athletes from [the home team] Basanga curiously came out of this catastrophe unscathed," reported the Kinshasa daily newspaper *L'Avenir*.

. . . .

According to an October 13, 2006, report in the *Wall Street Journal Asia*, golf camps in China, Japan, South Korea, and Singapore are teaching children as young as two years old. The report indicated that parents hope the children can be as financially successful as pro golfer Michelle Wie, who began playing at age four.

. . . .

BAILED BONDS

The baseball strike affected fans, owners, and players alike. It hit the fans emotionally, and it hit the owners and players financially. When the strike was in full force, San Francisco Giants outfielder Barry Bonds appeared before a San Francisco judge and requested that his child-support and alimony payments be cut in half. Bonds explained that when he was playing ball, he pulled in $4.75 million a year and paid out $15,000 a month in child support and alimony. But the strike put an end to his career highs, and now he was near the poverty level. The judge approved Bonds's request, cut his payments in half, and then shocked the court by asking for Bonds's autograph.

"Hitting is better than sex."

—Reggie Jackson, *Esquire*, March 1, 1978

GIVE ME A BREAK

In 1978, Jack Tatum of the Oakland Raiders made a "clothesline" hit on New England Patriots receiver Darryl Stingley. The hit broke Stingley's neck and caused permanent paralysis. Tatum not only didn't apologize for his maneuver, he also claimed it was a legal hit and warned other opponents they could expect the same. Nearly twenty years later, in January 1997, Tatum applied to the NFL Players Association for disability benefits of $156,000. He claimed that living with the fact that he had paralyzed someone had caused him mental anguish. How did he come up with the $156,000 figure? In the NFL Players Association, it is the highest category for compensation, the "catastrophic injury" category. Ironically, it's the same category that Stingley was in.

"It has options through the year 2020—or until the last Rocky movie is made."

—San Francisco Giants pitcher Dan Quisenberry, referring to his contract, *Major League Baseball Newsletter*, April 1990

NO SKIN OFF MY NOSE

At twenty-nine years old, and only 138 pounds, pugilist Con Orem agreed to a bare-knuckle boxing fight with 200-pound Hugh O'Neill. O'Neill, considered to be the toughest barroom brawler in the Montana Territory town of Virginia City, battled it out with the slender Orem for 185 rounds on January 3, 1865. Finally, the fight was ruled a draw.

· ·

While in the possession of the 1999 National Hockey League champions the Dallas Stars, the Stanley Cup acquired a mysterious and unexplained three-inch dent.

· ·

MIGHT AS WELL JUMP

In the third quarter of a game between the Cowboys and the Titans, Dallas Cowboys offensive lineman Andre Gurode had his helmet pulled off during a play. Titans defensive lineman Albert Haynesworth took advantage of the situation and stomped on Gurode's head. Haynesworth was ejected from the October 1, 2006, game, but not before shouting at the referee and at his own coach, Jeff Fisher. Why was Haynesworth so upset with Gurode? Because Gurode had successfully blocked Haynesworth on a play in which Dallas scored a touchdown. Gurode, who required numerous stitches on his face, did not return to the contest. Haynesworth was suspended for five games by the NFL.

> *"I don't mind getting beaten, but I hate to lose."*
>
> —Reggie Jackson, *Sepia*, March 1977

OFF BASE

On July 27, 1980, Montreal Expo Ron LeFlore had just stolen his sixty-second base on his way to an outrageous ninety-seven for the season, making him the first player to lead both leagues in stolen bases and pushing the Expos to second place, only one game behind the Philadelphia Phillies, who won the World Series. As the crowd cheered and LeFlore brushed himself off, he noticed the stadium's electronic scoreboard. He became engrossed in reading about the history of stolen bases and the fact that the first recorded steal had happened exactly 115 years ago to the day. With LeFlore basking in the glory of his achievement and his connection with baseball history, the pitcher fired the ball to second and picked him off.

"I'll play first, third, left. I'll play anywhere—except Philadelphia."

—Dick Allen (various teams), *Sporting News*, April 11, 1970

DROPPING YOUR GUARD

It's a play you won't find in any playbook. During a high school basketball game between Wadsworth and Copley High Schools in Ohio, a unique strategy was used to help maintain Copley's two-point lead. As a Wadsworth player prepared to throw an inbounds pass, a sixteen-year-old Copley student dove out of the stands and pulled down the player's shorts. The maneuver must have accomplished its goal since Copley went on to win the game 65–60, but the unidentified student was arrested as he tried to escape from the gymnasium. He was charged with disrupting a lawful meeting and disorderly conduct, both misdemeanors. The boy not only exposed his school's opponent, he also exposed himself to an unspecified number of days in suspension, and Principal Bill Steffen banned him from extracurricular activities. I wonder if the boy thought he was making a legitimate play—a drop shot, perhaps.

· ·

"If the Mets can win the World Series, the United States can get out of Vietnam."

—New York Mets pitcher Tom Seaver, in *Baseball's Greatest Quotations* by Paul Dickson (HarperResource, New York, 1991)

· ·

RAIN, RAIN, GO AWAY

Having games canceled because of inclement weather is nothing new or even noteworthy, except when it's a rainstorm so severe it cancels an *indoor* game. On June 15, 1976, in Texas, of course, where everything is supposedly bigger, the rains started just after the Houston and Pittsburgh players arrived at the Astrodome for early batting and fielding practice. Meteorologists reported as much as ten inches of rain in some areas of the city while the Astros and Pirates waited out the deluge inside the dome. But the rains kept umpires, stadium personnel, and fans from reaching the park. At 5:00 p.m. that day, even though a few die-hard fans had forged their way through the floods, the umpires and teams agreed to call off the game. With the rain still coming down outside, tables were brought onto the field, and the two teams ate dinner together.

Moments before being executed by lethal injection in a Huntsville, Texas, prison, on September 14, 1999, condemned murderer William Prince Davis said, "I'd like to say in closing: What about those Cowboys!"

FROZEN GAS

Quinnipiac College was leading Fairfield University 2–1 at the Wonderland of Ice arena in Bridgeport, Connecticut, and fans and players alike were pretty sick about the whole thing. It wasn't the score that turned everyone's stomach—it was the Zamboni machine. Apparently, an employee had forgotten to turn on the arena's exhaust fans when the ice-polishing machine entered the rink. Carbon monoxide fumes sent fourteen players to the hospital and canceled the game for the rest of the evening. I wonder if that's where the expression "You stink on ice" came from.

. . . .

On April 15, 1999, while taping a promotional spot for Texas agricultural products that was called the "Go Texan" campaign, encouraging consumers to purchase everything from Texas-grown apples to zucchini, legendary baseball pitcher Nolan Ryan threw pieces of fruit at a sheet of plexiglass situated in front of a camera. He threw one peach of a peach that missed the mark, hit a cameraman in the head, and knocked him to the ground.

. . . .

A LABOR-INTENSIVE SPORT

One pregnant woman from Detroit showed why her city is known as Hockeytown when she demanded to see the first game of the Stanley Cup finals even though she was going into labor. The woman began having contractions on her way to Joe Louis Arena, but she told her husband to keep going because she was determined to see the game. As her beloved Detroit Red Wings labored in their match over the Washington Capitals, the mother-to-be labored to keep her labor in check. To celebrate Detroit's 2–1 victory, the woman had a six-pound four-ounce daughter three hours after the game ended. I wonder if they decided to name the child in honor of the sport—"Zamboni," perhaps.

According to a June 6, 2006, report by ABC News, members of the New Salem, Alabama, Missionary Baptist Church voted 67-10 to fire pastor Stanley Hall because he refused to reschedule his consecration service even though it conflicted with the telecast of the Super Bowl.

BET YOU CAN'T DO THAT AGAIN!

At least eight golfers witnessed the most miraculous tee shot in golf history and have verified its authenticity. Todd Obuchowski got too much club behind his tee shot on the fourth hole at the Beaver Brook Golf Course in Haydenville, Massachusetts. The ball careened over the green of the 116-yard par-3 and onto a highway, hit the passenger side of a passing Toyota driven by Nancy Bachand, ricocheted back to the green, and rolled into the cup for a hole-in-one. Everyone was happy for the thirty-four-year-old metal worker, except the driver of the Toyota—her car suffered $150 in damages.

• •

As a goodwill gesture to their fans, the Houston Astros gave away all 54,350 tickets to the May 12, 1996, game against the Philadelphia Phillies, but only 30,828 people showed up.

• •

HOOP IN MOUTH DISEASE

When Christopher Conley of Nashua, New Hampshire, was playing a game of basketball, he charged the hoop, went up for a slam dunk, and got more hang time than he expected. His teeth got entangled in the net on the way down, and the fourteen-year-old went straight from the basketball court to a court of law. Conley and his parents sued Lifetime Products, the makers of the net, seeking damages for the cost of Christopher's extensive dental work. Lifetime Products settled with the Conleys in November 1995, and Christopher's technical foul netted him $50,000.

According to a November 9, 2001, Associated Press article, Buffalo Bills running back Travis Henry pled guilty to attempted sexual misconduct with a fifteen-year-old girl. The court sentenced him to one-hundred hours of community service and assigned him to Buffalo's St. Augustine Community Service Corp, where most of his duties consisted of counseling youths.

ALWAYS GOOD FOR A LAUGH

During a game between the Red Sox and the Philadelphia Athletics in September 1948, Boston's Billy Goodman came up to bat with Ted Williams on third. Goodman hit a bouncing grounder to A's shortstop Eddie Joost, who tried to scoop it up. The ball took an odd bounce, missed Joost's glove, rolled up his sleeve, and nestled somewhere in his jersey. A frantic Joost danced around the infield trying to bounce the ball loose. By the time he untucked his jersey and the ball finally made its appearance, it was too late to throw Goodman out at first. Fortunately, the disappearing-ball trick didn't cost the A's a run. Why? Because Williams was laughing so hard at Joost's antics he forgot to run home.

LANDING IN THE ROUGH

After a hard day on the links, Dale L. Larson was headed back to the clubhouse at the Indianhead Golf Course in Mosinee, Wisconsin, but he tripped on his golf spikes and fell face first onto the brick path. It took nine root canals and twenty-three dental crowns to get Larson's smile back to normal. He was so teed off that he sued the golf course for damages. During the trial, the jury agreed that the golf course was 51 percent responsible for Larson's accident. They concluded that if the path had been made of smooth concrete, Larson's golf spike might not have gotten stuck and he probably wouldn't have fallen. The court found Larson only 49 percent at fault for the accident. How could he be responsible for inferior conditions at the golf course? It was discovered that Larson had consumed thirteen drinks before the accident and had a 0.29 blood-alcohol level more than ninety minutes after his fall. The golf course appealed the decision, but in October 1996, Larson landed in the green when a Wisconsin appeals court upheld the trial court's award of $41,000. Just another case of the court system taking a slice out of common sense.

FIELD OF WEEDS

Groundskeepers at Anaheim Stadium were preparing the outfield for the California Angels home opener when they discovered grass sprouting everywhere. But the outfield is supposed to be covered in grass, right? Yes, but not this kind. The groundskeepers discovered nearly five-hundred baby marijuana plants sprouting in the field. It was deduced that the pot was accidentally seeded from fans of the rock group The Who, which played the stadium on March 21, 1976. Of the fifty-five thousand fans, about ten thousand were allowed to watch the concert from the outfield grass.

"A nickel ain't worth a dime anymore."

—Yogi Berra, *Baseball Digest*, June 1987

After successfully kicking a forty-three-yard field goal (his sixteenth of the year) against the New York Giants on December 15, 2001, Arizona Cardinals placekicker Bill Gramática leaped into the air in celebration and ruptured his anterior cruciate ligament (ACL) when he landed, ending his season and jeopardizing his career.

THAT'S A LONG, LONG TIME

Most people interested in boxing have heard of the notorious Battle of the Long Count between world heavyweight champion Gene Tunney and former champion Jack Dempsey on September 22, 1927. But before that legendary event, there was an even longer count, and this one was much more than just a few additional seconds. On January 7, 1920, Jack McAuliffe was refereeing a fight between Jimmy O'Gatty and Packey McFarland. O'Gatty had dropped McFarland to the mat four times, but the ref never even started the count—each time he waited for the flattened McFarland to rise. Ringsiders began wondering if McAuliffe might be in someone's pocket, and their suspicions were confirmed on the fifth knockdown when McFarland lay unconscious for a full ten minutes. Finally, McAuliffe declared O'Gatty the winner.

ACCORDING TO A MAY 17, 2002, REUTERS ARTICLE, TWENTY-SEVEN BRITISH MEN WITH OUTSTANDING ARREST WARRANTS VOLUNTARILY TURNED THEMSELVES IN TO POLICE. THE MEN KNEW THEY WOULD ONLY SERVE A SHORT SENTENCE, AND THEY DIDN'T WANT TO BE ARRESTED LATER AND MISS WATCHING THE WORLD CUP MATCHES SINCE JAILS IN HERTFORDSHIRE, ENGLAND, DON'T HAVE TELEVISION SETS.

PLAY-BY-NUMBERS SET

The old barker's line, "You can't tell one player from the other without a program" wasn't true in the early days of college football because they didn't even have numbers on their jerseys. It wasn't until December 5, 1908, that the University of Pittsburgh introduced the exciting innovation of putting numbers on its players' jerseys. Unfortunately for the Panthers, those would be the only numbers they put on that day. They lost to the Washington & Jefferson Presidents, 14–0.

. . . .

Najeh Davenport, running back for the Green Bay Packers, accepted community service to settle a charge that he broke into a university dormitory. According to an October 29, 2002, Associated Press article, Davenport was accused not only of breaking into the dormitory but also of defecating in a woman's wardrobe closet.

. . . .

HE'S A REAL KNOCKOUT

Knockouts are nothing special in the sport of boxing—unless, of course, you knock yourself out. That is exactly what happened on September 27, 1938, when Eddie Phillips won by a KO without ever laying a glove on his opponent. Phillips was in the ring in Harringay, North London, against Irish heavyweight Jack "The Irish Thrush" Doyle (nicknamed "Irish Thrush" because he sang better than he fought). In the second round, Doyle rushed Phillips and mistimed his roundhouse right punch. He completely missed Phillips's face, and the momentum of the swing catapulted Doyle past Phillips and over the top of the ropes. Doyle landed headfirst on the ring apron, knocking himself out cold. Eight months later, the rematch gave Phillips the opportunity to do to Doyle what Doyle had done to himself—knock him out in the first round.

. . . .

"Did you hear that? I didn't hear anything. Put that question another way."
—Major League Baseball Hall of Famer Ernie Banks,
Sports Illustrated, August 23, 1982

. . . .

THE NAME
OF THE GAME

Baseball Teams from the International League (1884–Present)

1890, GRAND RAPIDS SHAMROCKS

1887–1889, HAMILTON HAMS

1954–1960, HAVANA SUGAR KINGS

2008–PRESENT, LEHIGH VALLEY IRONPIGS

1888–1890, LONDON TECUMSEHS

2002–PRESENT, LOUISVILLE BATS

If you think these names for baseball teams are interesting, wait until you hear about these players' names. According to an August 18, 2006, article in the Orlando Sentinel, Yourhighness Morgan was a linebacker for South Sumter High School in Bushnell, Florida. His brother's name is Handsome Morgan, and his cousin's name is Gorgeous Morgan.

SAY CHEESE!

Whenever you see the Green Bay Packers playing football, you're bound to see some fans wearing big foam-rubber pieces of cheese on their heads. Wisconsin is cheese territory, and the cheeseheads take their *fromage* seriously. So seriously, in fact, that two makers of the cheese chapeau have taken each other to court. The original maker of the novelty hat, Foamation, Inc., has sued its cheesy rival, Scofield Souvenir & Postcard Company, of Menomonee Falls, for copyright infringement, trademark infringement, and unfair competition. Scofield, which cut the cheese profits of Foamation, countersued for, among other things, tortuous interference with a business contract, libel, and defamation. It seems like there isn't enough cheese to spread around.

A HEAD OF THE GAME

When Craig "MacT" MacTavish, center for the St. Louis Blues NHL hockey team, announced his retirement in 1997, it was the end of an era. MacTavish joined the league in 1978, the year before wearing helmets was mandatory, and he was the last player to play helmetless. He was allowed to decide whether to use a helmet or not since he qualified for a grandfather clause, and he chose not to wear one, calling it "a comfort thing." Although he played helmetless for seventeen years, he never was seriously hurt.

. . . .

The *Chicago Tribune* reported on July 17, 2007, that NHL player Derek Boogaard (left winger who played for the Minnesota Wild and the New York Rangers), known primarily as a fighter and enforcer, opened the Derek and Aaron Boogaard Fighting Camp in Regina, Saskatchewan. The purpose of the fighting camp was to train and encourage teenage hockey players in that violent but crucial hockey skill.

. . . .

DOUBLEDAY DOUBLE PLAY

When asked about who invented baseball, most people believe the answer is Abner Doubleday, and most people would be wrong. Baseball was invented in England (gasp!) and first described in 1744 in *A Little Pretty Pocket-Book,* which was reprinted in the United States in 1762. So how did Abner Doubleday get credit for inventing a game that had been around for nearly a hundred years? It was a propaganda campaign. The major league executive board, wanting to score a home run by claiming baseball had been invented in America, commissioned a report on the game's origin in 1907. This is the report that first credited baseball as the brainchild of Civil War general and hero Abner Doubleday in Cooperstown, New York, in 1839, even though Doubleday never mentioned inventing baseball in his diaries, nor did he ever visit Cooperstown. Makes you wonder about the origins of apple pie and Chevrolet now, doesn't it?

BASES LOADED

So who should get credit for inventing baseball? Most authorities now agree that Alexander Cartwright, a Manhattan bookseller, should get the credit for inventing the modern game of baseball. He founded the Knickerbocker Base Ball Club in 1842, named after the Knickerbocker Fire Engine Company for which he was a volunteer. Cartwright drew the first diagram of the diamond-shaped field, and the rules of the modern game are based on bylaws his team created. He was inducted into the National Baseball Hall of Fame in 1938.

. . . .

In the thirty-seventh Tour de France in 1950, Algerian-French cyclist Abdel-Kader Zaaf drank a bottle of wine, purportedly to ward off the intense heat, and promptly fell off his bike. After sleeping it off by the side of the road, he got back on and rode off—in the wrong direction.

. . . .

THEIR CROSS TO BEAR

Jean de Brébeuf, a French Jesuit missionary, was watching some Huron Indians of southeastern Canada play a unique game called *baaga'adowe* (meaning "they bump hips") during his stay in 1636. He wrote in his journal that the players used curved sticks with net pouches on the end to toss a small ball back and forth to one another. Since de Brébeuf was a very religious man, he observed that the stick looked strikingly similar to the cross carried by French bishops, called a crosier, or *la crosse*. De Brébeuf's writings are the first documented mention of the game lacrosse and the origin of the modern name.

. . . .

"You can't compare me to my father (Yogi Berra). Our similarities are different."
—Dale Berra, *Sports Illustrated*, August 9, 1982

. . . .

TACKLING DISCRIMINATION

In 1989, Francis Scott Key High School in Union Bridge, Maryland, was under pressure from a new federal statute that banned school discrimination in sports on the basis of gender. The school board was afraid if it disallowed anyone from participating in sports because of his or her sex, it would be setting itself up for a major lawsuit. That's how seventeen-year-old Tawana Hammond became the first female running back in the school's history. Unfortunately, she didn't make it past the first scrimmage. When she was tackled during the first play, she fell on the knees of an opposing player, was seriously hurt, and eventually suffered the loss of half her pancreas.

In October 1992, Tawana Hammond filed a lawsuit against the Carroll County Board of Education for $1.5 million on the grounds that no one explained to her "the potential risks of serious and disabling injury inherent in the sport." An example of unsportswoman-like conduct, or just someone who has never watched *Monday Night Football*? You make the call.

ONLY THE GOOD PLAY YOUNG

During his senior season on the Harrodsburg (Kentucky) High School football team, Dennis Johnson, who later became an Arizona Cardinals and San Francisco 49ers defensive end, was named National Player of the Year by *Sports Illustrated*. *USA Today*, *Sporting News*, and *Parade* named him National High School Football Defensive Player of the Year for 1997. That's interesting, of course, but not as interesting as the fact that Johnson began his high school football career at age 6 as a five-foot-seven, 170-pound second-grader, according to an April 9, 2002, profile in the *Los Angeles Times*. The national rules have changed since then, and now only ninth-graders and older can play.

RUNNING OUT OF PATIENCE

"I laughed, but I felt like crying," said South Africa's Johannes Coleman after being told his new world record could not be validated. "It must have been my fastest ever marathon." The marathon he's talking about was the 1938 Natal Marathon at Alexander Park, Pietermaritzburg (South Africa). At that time, the world record time stood at two hours, twenty-six minutes, forty seconds, and as Coleman entered the park, his own watch indicated he had beaten the record by three minutes. He was expecting accolades, but all he got was complete silence—the judges weren't there. He wandered around looking for them and finally discovered chief timekeeper Harold Sulin drinking tea with colleagues in the refreshment room. They apologized profusely to the nearly exhausted runner and explained that they weren't at their position because they didn't think anyone would finish the race that early, so his time couldn't be verified. Although Coleman was a British Empire Games Marathon gold medal winner that same year, he never again managed to get close to breaking the world record.

"NEVES, CALLED DEAD IN FALL, DENIES IT."

—*San Francisco Examiner*
headline, May 8, 1936

On May 8, 1936, during the fifth race of the program at the Bay
Meadows Racetrack in San Mateo, California, nineteen-year-old
jockey Ralph Neves was thrown from his mount, Flannikins, and
trampled by several horses. He was pronounced dead, and track
announcer Oscar Otis announced the news to the stunned crowd
and asked for a moment of silence. The body was removed from
the track and placed in the morgue at nearby Mills Memorial
Hospital. Neves's friend Dr. Horace Stevens decided to give
him an adrenaline shot to the heart and, surprisingly, Neves
awakened. He stumbled out of the hospital and, wearing only
a hospital gown and his boots, hailed a cab and made it back to
the racetrack. He demanded to ride the rest of his mounts in the
program, but officials refused to let him ride until the next day.

FAST AND FURIOUS RIDE

On June 6, 1968, at the Smokey Mountain Raceway near Maryville, Tennessee, driver Buddy Baker's car blew a tire. His Dodge spun out of control, slammed into a cement wall at the first turn, flipped upside down, and landed near a creek. An ambulance soon arrived, and the driver cut Baker's seat belt, causing Baker to land on his head. Though Baker protested getting into the ambulance, the driver was adamant and quickly strapped Baker to a gurney. As he pulled out with sirens blaring, the unfastened back doors opened and Baker, still strapped to the gurney, flew out and rolled onto the track. Fortunately, the other drivers were under the yellow caution flag and were able to steer around him. Baker survived this incident relatively unharmed and went on to win nineteen NASCAR races, including the prestigious Daytona 500 in 1980 (still the record for fastest Daytona 500 ever run at an average speed of 177.602 miles per hour).

SLEIGHT OF HAND

Joel Youngblood, center fielder for the New York Mets, showed up at historic Wrigley Field in Chicago on August 4, 1982, not knowing he would wind up in the history books. In the third inning, he hit a two-run single off the Cubs' Ferguson Jenkins. Mets manager George Bamberger congratulated him and then told him something else—he had been traded to the Montreal Expos—and they wanted him right away. So Youngblood grabbed his gear and caught a plane to Philadelphia to join the Expos' lineup late in the game. Even with the pressure to make it to the game, Youngblood was able to single off Phillies ace Steve Carlton, making him the only player in baseball history to be on two different teams, bat against two future Hall of Famers, and get hits off both of them—all in the same day.

"I'LL NEVER FORGET SEPTEMBER SIXTH NINETEEN-FIFTY. I GOT A LETTER THREATENING ME, HANK BAUER, YOGI BERRA AND JOHNNY MIZE. IT SAID IF I SHOWED UP IN UNIFORM AGAINST THE RED SOX I'D BE SHOT. I TURNED THE LETTER OVER TO THE FBI AND TOLD MY MANAGER CASEY STENGEL ABOUT IT. YOU KNOW WHAT CASEY DID? HE GAVE ME A DIFFERENT UNIFORM AND GAVE MINE TO BILLY MARTIN. CAN YOU IMAGINE THAT! GUESS CASEY THOUGHT IT'D BE BETTER IF BILLY GOT SHOT."

—Phil Rizzuto, *Sport* magazine, December 1961

SIGHT UNSEEN

At the Olney Alleys in Philadelphia, on December 6, 1933, professional bowler Bill Knox attempted to demonstrate the art of "spot bowling" to fans. He had two pin boys hold a screen about one foot off the lane above the foul line. He wanted to show the best way to bowl by using the spots on the lane and not by aiming at the pins. To everyone's amazement, including his own, Knox bowled twelve consecutive strikes without ever seeing the pins—a perfect game. What made the feat more incredible was that, until that time, Knox had never bowled a perfect game in his life.

. . . .

In the nineteenth century, a number of cities in the United States banned nine-pin bowling, which was the standard at that time, because of its association with gambling and organized crime. An enterprising fan had the idea of adding another pin, and so the ten-pin bowling game we know today was invented and eventually led to the creation of the American Bowling Congress in 1895.

. . . .

PUTTING THE CART BEFORE THE HEARSE

Charleston, West Virginia, native Diana J. Nagy filed a lawsuit against the makers of a golf cart for contributing to the death of her husband. Mr. Nagy, who had been drinking heavily during a golf tournament at the Berry Hills Country Club, fell out of the cart and died. Mrs. Nagy claimed negligence on the part of the cart manufacturer for not having seat belts and doors on the carts. She also named her son in the lawsuit, since he was driving the cart at the time.

. . . .

Southpaw Joe Nuxhall of the Cincinnati Reds hurled his first major league game on June 10, 1944, and set a yet unbeaten record. At fifteen years, ten months, and eleven days of age, Nuxhall is the youngest player ever to appear in a major league game.

. . . .

BAD, BAD SPORTSMANSHIP

The world of sports has always had its bad boys—players who purposely try to injure their opponents by hitting them with a clothesline, biting off an ear, or high-sticking. If you think the world of sports has gotten more violent over the years, and that in the early days, people were more sportsmanlike, think again. On May 29, 1606, the Italian painter Caravaggio was playing tennis against Ranuccio Tomassoni, and an argument broke out over a close line call. Both men disputed the call, and their verbal exchanges got more and more heated. Caravaggio stormed off the court, returned shortly with a pistol, and shot Tomassoni to death. So are players meaner today than they were in the past? That's your call.

SHORTEST DISTANCE POSSIBLE

On April 21, 1980, Rosie Ruiz finished the eighty-fourth Boston Marathon in the female world record time of two hours, thirty-one minutes, and fifty-six seconds. But suspicions were aroused when spectators noted that the twenty-six-year-old New Yorker didn't seem winded and wasn't sweating. When questioned about the route she was supposed to have taken, Ruiz didn't recall any of the highlights (like the cheering students of Wellesley College) and, to top it off, no one could recall seeing her in the race. According to an article in the May 5, 1980, *Sports Illustrated*, Ruiz, who had finished the New York Marathon in 1979, was investigated and disqualified after an eyewitness saw her on the subway during that race on the way to the finish line. Later that week, the Boston Athletic Association also disqualified Ruiz. Her propensity for fraud didn't stop there; in 1982, she was arrested for embezzling $60,000 from a real estate company for which she worked, and then, in 1983, she was arrested in Miami, Florida, for her involvement in a cocaine deal.

BETWEEN A ROCK AND A HARD PLACE

In 1955, Gary Player was in the lead on the final hole at England's Huddersfield Golf Club and only needed a par-4 to win. He chipped his second shot, and it landed near the green only a few inches from a stone wall. The lie of the ball gave him no room for a backswing, and he didn't want to lose a stroke tapping it clear of the wall. So Player decided to ricochet the ball off the wall. The physics seemed simple enough, but things didn't work out the way he had planned. The ball bounced off the wall and hit Player square in the face. Not only did he suffer the pain and humiliation of getting struck with his own ball, he was also penalized two strokes for impeding the flight of the ball. He lost the tournament.

OUT FOR GOOD

Too many players to count have been sent to the penalty box, or suspended for a game or a season, but there's only one NHL player ever banned from the game for life—Billy Coutu. At the end of game four of the 1927 Stanley Cup, Coutu assaulted referee Jerry Laflamme and tackled referee Billy Bell, causing a bench-clearing brawl between the Boston Bruins and Ottawa Senators. On October 8, 1929, the suspension was lifted so Coutu could play in the minor leagues; however, he never played in the NHL again.

The Baltimore Orioles have had their name since 1954; but from 1895 to 1896, they were called the Milwaukee Creams.

BAD BOY OF HOCKEY

Chicago Blackhawks forward Patrick Kane and his cousin were arrested on August 9, 2009, in Buffalo, New York, for robbing and assaulting a taxi driver over exact change. The two passengers became enraged when the cab driver didn't have the 20 cents change to give them for the $14.80 cab fare they paid with $15.00. They were accused of punching the cab driver in the face and head, breaking his glasses, and grabbing him by the throat. They then pried the $15 they paid the driver out of his hand and fled the scene. They were eventually apprehended around 5:00 a.m.

. . . .

Before 1967, it wasn't illegal for Olympic athletes to use drugs to enhance their performance during competition.

. . . .

ONE-ARMED BANDIT

When a fighter is declared the winner, the referee traditionally raises the boxer's arm in victory. When Tommy Rodgers knocked down Somersby Dowst in an NCAA championship bout in Cambridge, Massachusetts, on March 27, 1947, the ref didn't have a choice about which of Rodgers' arms to raise—he only had one. The one-armed Rodgers, who twice knocked down Dowst during their title bout, was declared the winner in the ninth round.

• •

No network footage exists of Super Bowl I on January 15, 1967, between the NFL champion Green Bay Packers and the AFL champion Kansas City Chiefs, who were defeated 35–10. Why? Supposedly, the tape was reused to record a soap opera.

• •

LIKE WHITE ON RICE

Jackie Robinson famously broke the color barrier in baseball, and soon nearly every sport followed suit. But the Professional Golfers' Association of America was in line to get a black eye because it was slow to follow through with integrating the links. In fact, it wasn't until November 9, 1961, when the PGA finally voted to eliminate from its constitution the clause specifying that all of its members be Caucasian.

. . . .

Forty-six-year-old Christophe Fauviau, of Mont-de-Marsan, France, was found guilty and sentenced to eight years in prison in the death of a young tennis player. Reuters reported on March 2, 2006, that Fauviau admitted to spiking the sports drinks of twenty-seven young players with a tranquilizer in hopes of giving his son, Maxime, and his daughter, Valentine, an advantage during their tournament matches.

. . . .

OUT OF THIS WORLD

Former major league baseball all-star catcher Darren "Dutch" Daulton (Phillies and Marlins), who retired in 1997, told the *Philadelphia Daily News* on February 2, 2006, that he now understands alternate dimensions of reality. He wasn't talking about his several arrests, his probation, his two-month incarceration in the Pinellas County Jail, his divorce from his Playboy model wife, Nicole, or even his second divorce. Dutch was talking about the supernatural, the Mayan calendar, dimensions of time and space, the occult, and numerology (he's obsessed with the number eleven). He claims he first experienced his other-earthly powers after he broke into tears following a game-winning hit in the 1990s, when he realized, "I didn't hit that ball. Something happened, but it wasn't me." It's okay if you don't subscribe to Daulton's beliefs. He said everything would be proven on December 21, 2012, at 11:11 a.m. Greenwich mean time. In 2007, Daulton authored a book on occultism and numerology, titled *If They Only Knew.*

LOST IN TRANSLATION

An apparently sober twenty-five-year-old American from Boston was in Hanover, Germany, for World Cup soccer matches when he was compelled to visit local police because he couldn't remember the name of the hotel he had checked into or even where it was located. According to a June 23, 2006, Reuters article, the only landmarks the man could remember was that the hotel was near a park and a Mercedes dealership, and since he was in Germany, there were plenty of both. Police kindly drove him around town for an hour until the man eventually spotted his hotel.

. . . .

The Associated Press reported on lawyer Michael Oddenino's $3 million lawsuit against the coach of his daughter's high school softball team in Arcadia, California. The March 30, 2006, article reported that Oddenino was suing for his daughter's emotional distress because the coach called her a two-year-old and referred to the entire team as idiots after members made minor mistakes. The case was rejected.

. . . .

TRY, TRY AGAIN

Beltran de Osorio y Diez de Rivera, the eighteenth Duke of Albuquerque and courtier to the Spanish royal family, received a film of England's Grand National Steeplechase horse race, and at age eight became obsessed with winning that race. On his first attempt, in 1952, the "Iron" Duke fell from his horse; he regained consciousness in a hospital suffering from a cracked vertebra. In 1963, with the odds against him at 66–1, the duke fell from his mount once again. In 1965, he broke his leg after he fell from his collapsed horse. In 1974, while training for the Grand National and recovering from having sixteen screws removed from a leg he had shattered in another race, the duke fell again, and this time broke his collarbone. He recovered in time to compete and actually managed to finish the race while still on his horse, although he rode wearing a plaster cast. It was the only race he ever finished, in eighth place. Then in 1976, he fell during another race, and this time he was trampled by the other horses. He suffered several injuries, including seven broken ribs, several broken vertebrae, a broken wrist, a broken thigh, and a severe concussion that left him in a coma for two days. At fifty-seven years of age, the emotionally and physically shattered duke announced that he was going to have another go at the Grand National. For his own safety, race organizers pulled the duke's racing license. Although he never fulfilled his dream of winning the Grand National, he did set one record—he broke more bones attempting to win than any jockey before or since.

IT IS REPORTED THAT DURING THE DUKE'S 1974 ATTEMPT, HE BUMPED INTO RIDER RON BARRY AT THE SECOND CANAL TURN. BARRY TURNED ANGRILY AND ASKED, "WHAT THE ** ARE YOU DOING?" THE DUKE REPLIED, "MY DEAR CHAP, I HAVEN'T A CLUE. I'VE NEVER GOT THIS FAR BEFORE!"**

THE COURT OF NO RETURN

On January 19, 1977, University of Cincinnati guard Brian Williams had a shot that dreams are made of. He was all alone, dribbling full speed down the court to an unprotected basket and planning on making a fabulous, highlight-reel dunk. He was so excited about the anticipated glory that he misjudged his takeoff point and began to descend before getting to the rim. He strained with all of his might to get as close to the basket as possible, but he just couldn't make it. Not only did he miss the shot, he also missed the basket and the net. The only thing he didn't miss was slamming the ball off the head of referee Darrin Brown, who was standing under the basket. Williams is credited with having the only slam-dunk air ball in basketball history.

. . . .

Until the 1870s, baseball was played without the use of gloves. Doug Allison, a catcher for the Cincinnati Red Stockings, is credited as the first player to use one, and he did that only because he had an injured left hand.

. . . .

A SERIOUS WEIGHT PROBLEM

Henry Armstrong was a boxing chameleon. In October 1937, Armstrong won the featherweight title (weighing 126 pounds) by knocking out Petey Sarron. About half a year later, in May, Armstrong was able to gain enough weight (weighing 147 pounds) to compete in the welterweight division and took the title from Barney Ross. Then, on August 17, 1938, Armstrong dropped down to 135 pounds to compete in the lightweight division and take the crown away from champ Lou Ambers. Armstrong has the distinction of being the only fighter in the sport's history to simultaneously hold the championship belts of three different weight classifications.

• •

The Toronto newspaper *Globe and Mail* reported on November 30, 2006, that professional darts player Robbie "Kong" Green had been suspended for eight weeks after a positive drug test. Britain's Darts Regulatory Authority announced Green's suspension after he tested positive for marijuana.

• •

MAKING BOND

It was an exciting day on October 7, 2001, when San Francisco Giants slugger Barry Bonds hit his seventy-third home run into the stands. But the excitement didn't stop there. Alex Popov, a health-food restaurant owner from Berkeley, California, reached out with his glove, and the ball landed in it, but for only six-tenths of a second before it bounced out and was snagged by Patrick Hayashi, a college student from San Diego. Hayashi was escorted by security guards to a room where officials authenticated the ball as genuine and certified him as the owner. But Popov wasn't giving up, and he sued Hayashi for return of the ball. The case didn't go to court for more than a year, and following a two-week trial, the judge deliberated for an entire month before reaching his decision. In a judgment that would make King Solomon proud, the judge ruled that both men were legitimate owners and ordered that the ball be sold at auction and the proceeds split evenly between the two men. It was estimated that the ball could fetch as much as $2 million, but it eventually sold for only $450,000, meaning that each man would get $225,000. But for all his troubles, Popov wound up getting much less. In fact, he got less than zero because he had to pay his attorney fees. In July 2003, he was sued for $473,500 in unpaid legal bills relating to his claim.

IT WAS ALMOST ALL GREEK TO THEM

In the first modern-day Olympics in 1896, officially known as the Games of the I Olympiad, Athens-born runner Spyridon Belokas became a national hero when he and two fellow Greeks took the top three spots in the marathon race. Belokas crossed the finish line behind Spiridon Louis and Kharilaos Vasilakos, winning the bronze and the admiration of his country. But shortly after the race, Belokas admitted to hitching a ride in a horse-drawn carriage during the race and was disqualified. He was stripped of his medal and other accolades, and he became a national disgrace overnight. Gyula Kellner, a Hungarian, was awarded third place.

RIVERSIDE COUNTY, CALIFORNIA, JUDGE PAUL E. ZELLERBACH WAS ADMONISHED BY THE STATE'S JUDICIAL AGENCY STEMMING FROM CONDUCT DURING AN OCTOBER 2004 CASE. ACCORDING TO AN AUGUST 16, 2006, ARTICLE IN THE *INLAND VALLEY DAILY BULLETIN*, ZELLERBACH EXCUSED HIMSELF WHILE THE JURY WAS DELIBERATING A MURDER CHARGE IN ORDER TO ATTEND AN ANGELS–RED SOX PLAYOFF GAME. HE REFUSED TO LEAVE THE GAME EVEN AFTER BEING NOTIFIED THAT THE JURY HAD REACHED ITS DECISION, THEREBY FORCING EVERYONE ASSOCIATED WITH THE CASE TO RETURN THE NEXT DAY.

TALK ABOUT A CLUB FOOT

The British Boxing Board of Control said it had no choice but to award the victory to Tony Wilson over Steve McCarthy in a light-heavyweight bout that occurred on September 21, 1989, despite "the unsatisfactory nature of the ending of this contest." In the third round, McCarthy sent Wilson to the canvas for an eight count, and then pummeled him against the ropes when he got up. The fans were on their feet, but one fan had taken something off her feet—her high-heeled shoes. Wilson's sixty-two-year-old mom, Minna, suddenly appeared in the ring brandishing her shoes and repeatedly clonking McCarthy over the head with them, opening up a wound on his scalp. The referee stopped the bout for a few minutes, then ordered McCarthy and Wilson to resume fighting. McCarthy refused to continue and was disqualified. The board stressed that a rematch between the two boxers would be held at a different venue, produced by a different promoter, under tighter security, and without Mrs. Wilson.

"A guy that throws what he intends to throw, that's the definition of a good pitcher."

—Former Los Angeles Dodger Sandy Koufax,
Los Angeles Times, March 31, 1971

GRADY'S GREATEST GOOF

Baseball is filled with unbelievable feats and records worthy of breaking, except in the case of Mike Grady, third baseman for the New York Giants. Grady holds the record no one wants to break: four errors committed on a single play. In 1899, Grady tried to field a routine ground ball, but bobbled it (error number one). He threw the ball to first, but it went sailing over the first baseman's head (error number two). The first baseman retrieved the ball and fired it back to Grady as the runner rounded second; Grady missed (error number three). Grady chased the ball as it rolled to the dugout, scooped it up, and zinged it to the catcher, but missed him by a mile (error number four). This final error allowed the runner to score on what should have been an easy out at first. Grady became the biggest goat in baseball—but only for a short time.

. . . .

"When I began playing the game, baseball was about as gentlemanly as a kick in the crotch."

—Ty Cobb, *The Giants of the Polo Grounds*, by Noel Hynd (Doubleday, New York, 1988)

. . . .

PARADISE REGAINED

Less than a year later, Grady and teammates Kid Gleason (future manager of the infamous Black Sox) and George Davis were walking to the Polo Grounds in New York City for their game when they saw smoke and flames rising from an apartment building. Davis quickly scurried up a fire escape and rescued a woman from the third floor. Grady and Gleason bolted up to the fourth floor, saving the life of a Mrs. Tibbets and her three-year-old, bringing them safely to the ground. Then Grady ran back up to the third floor and helped rescue a Mrs. Pease. The three players then made their way to the ballpark, where they tied the Boston Beaneaters, 10–10. Three saves, no errors.

. . . .

"They said I was such a great prospect that they were sending me to a winter league to sharpen up. When I stepped off the plane, I was in Greenland."

—Bob Uecker, *Baseball Digest*, June 1972

. . . .

CALL 'EM LIKE
I SEE 'EM

According to a March 31, 2006, Reuters article, the Nigerian Football (soccer) Association informed its referees that if they were offered a bribe, it would be all right to accept it. The article commented that bribery is considered acceptable behavior in Nigeria. However, they warned that the referees shouldn't go through with their part of the bargain and should only pretend they would treat the briber favorably since they had an obligation to call a game fairly.

• •

Ah, nuts! Terra Linda High School (San Rafael, California) senior D. J. Saint James was featured in a February 14, 2006, article in the *Marin Independent Journal* for his sterling record on the school's wrestling team. The profile highlighted one of Saint James's freshman matches in which he suffered a ruptured testicle that had swollen to the size of a fist and needed to be removed. But before Saint James left the mat to seek medical attention, he was able to tough it out long enough to pin his opponent.

• •

MORE NAME GAMES

Baseball Teams from the International League (1884–Present)

1918–1933, JERSEY CITY SKEETERS

1984–1988, MAINE GUIDES

1891–1892, NEW HAVEN NUTMEGS

1902–1907, NEWARK SAILORS

1886–1887, OSWEGO STARCHBOXES

1885, OSWEGO SWEEGS

ENGLISH SOCCER PLAYER GLEN JOHNSON—WHO EARNS THE AMERICAN EQUIVALENT OF $58,000 A WEEK, ACCORDING TO THE *GUARDIAN*—WAS ARRESTED ON JANUARY 19, 2007, AT A B&Q STORE IN DARTFORD, ENGLAND. JOHNSON WAS CAUGHT BY A SECURITY GUARD, WHO SPOTTED THE DEFENDER SWITCHING A HIGH-PRICED TOILET SEAT INTO THE BOX OF A CHEAPER ONE.

THE EYES HAVE IT

The traditional taunt to a referee that "you're blind" was only half true in the case of Big Ten conference football referee James Filson. In 2005, a reporter disclosed that Filson had been officiating games with only one eye following an accident in 2000 that left him with a prosthetic eye. After a golf outing in Miami, thirteen-year Big Ten veteran Filson tripped over a step and fell face first into the corner of a table, basically destroying his right eye. According to a July 18, 2006, article in the *Chicago Sun-Times*, he was fired after the incident was uncovered, and he soon filed a lawsuit. In his defense, Filson pointed out that he had been officiating with one eye for nearly five years, and those who grade officials rated Filson higher in his five seasons with one eye than in his eight seasons with two eyes. But the conference countered, saying that now the word was out, he would be overly criticized on close calls.

HURLING A BALL

An October 26, 1998, article in the *New England Journal of Medicine* reported on what apparently was the first ever and hopefully last ever transfer of a food-poisoning virus in any kind of sport. This happened during the September 19, 1998, football game between Florida State and Duke. Even though Duke lost 62–13, they must have felt some sense of revenge after forty-three nauseous Duke players and assistants inadvertently made eleven FSU players violently ill during and after the game. Game films showed sick Duke players with vomit on their jerseys making contact with opponents, wiping their virus laden mouthpieces on their hands, then touching and even shaking hands with FSU players. The source of the virus was traced to contaminated turkey sandwiches in a box lunch the assistants and team had eaten the day before.

WEIGHT WATCHERS

South African boxer Thomas Hamilton-Brown narrowly lost a split decision to Carlos Lillo on December 6, 1936, during the Summer Olympics in Berlin. This defeat knocked him out of the competition for an Olympic gold medal. To say the least, he was distraught. He decided the only way to make himself feel better would be to go on an eating binge—and boy, he sure did. Hamilton-Brown was pounding it away when his manager found him and explained there had been a scoring error and the judges had awarded him the split decision. But when Hamilton-Brown went back for the weigh-in for the next round, he had put on five pounds during his eating extravaganza. The extra pounds pushed him over the Olympic weight limit, and he was disqualified for the next fight.

. . . .

"Anybody with ability can play in the big leagues. To last as long as I did with the skills I had, with the numbers I produced, was a triumph of the human spirit."

—Bob Uecker, *Catcher in the Wry*, by Bob Uecker
(G. P. Putnam's Sons, New York, 1982)

. . . .

SHAKE THAT THANG

Pom-pons are also known as pompons, pom-poms, pompoms, and poms, since they all derive from the French word *pompon* (typically, a small, decorative ball made of feathers or fabric). All the spellings ending in "n" are the official names; the spellings ending in "m" are the more popular versions. The history of the pom-pon can be traced back to the 1930s, when they were all handmade from paper. Then in 1953, Lawrence Herkimer founded the Cheerleading Supply Company and started commercially manufacturing pom-pons. But it wasn't until 1965, when Fred Gastoff invented the first vinyl pom-pons used by the International Cheerleading Foundation, that pom-pons became a staple of the cheerleading world. Rah, rah, rah.

· ·

In 2000, a fan paid $8,000 for a pair of Ty Cobb's false teeth.

· ·

STOP FOOLING AROUND

The *Houston Chronicle* reported on January 22, 2006, that referee John Hampton called a technical foul on University of Houston basketball coach Tom Penders after Penders crumpled to his hands and knees on the court with 52.6 seconds to play in the first half. The referee thought Hampton was mocking him for previously calling a foul on Penders's team. But Penders, who ha a history of heart problems and wears a pacemaker, was sufferin a dizzy spell and had to be taken off the court on a stretcher. Referee Hampton refused to rescind the penalty.

NICKNAME GIVEN TO SWIMMER MICHAEL PHELPS—ALL-TIME RECORD HOLDER WITH EIGHTEEN OLYMPIC GOLD MEDALS—BY HIS OLYMPICS TEAMMATES: "GOMER."

A TOSS
AND A PRAYER

It seems that sometimes the sports gods do interfere with the work of mortal men. Case in point: The clock was winding down with the score at 77 all between the Florida State Seminoles and the Fighting Gobblers of Virginia Tech during their January 21, 1980, game. Florida State heaved the final shot, which bounced off the rim and caromed haphazardly toward the corner. Virginia Tech forward Les Henson captured the ball, turned, and chucked it toward the basket on the other side of the court and . . . it went through. The Gobblers gobbled up an amazing victory and Henson went down in the history books. An analysis of the throw showed that Henson had heaved the ball eighty-nine feet, three inches, the second-longest shot ever made in competition.

. . . .

On February 7, 1985, Marshall University's Bruce Morris beat Henson's record by making a basket from eighty-nine feet, ten inches out.

. . . .

WAVE YOUR HANDS IN THE AIR LIKE YOU JUST DON'T CARE

The finish line was in sight, and Alex Wilson of Canada was sure he had won gold in the men's 800-meter final during the 1932 Olympic Games in Los Angeles. A yard before he stepped over the line, he threw his arms up in a celebratory gesture and was all smiles. However, his smile quickly disappeared. Wilson, so confident he had won, slowed his pace slightly during his premature celebration, and it was enough time for Britain's Tommy Hampson to pass him at the last second and take the first-place position.

. . . .

In the United States, the most likely place where one might suffer an alligator attack is not in a swamp but on a golf course.

. . . .

I LOVE YOU, SO SUE ME

In 1998, Lyons Partnership, the owners of Barney the purple dinosaur, filed a copyright and trademark infringement suit against Ted Giannoulas, the Famous Chicken of San Diego. The suit claimed that the Famous Chicken performed repeated skits in which he assaulted a Barney-like character. The court, however, ruled that Giannoulas's performance was protected as a legitimate parody, and he was not only victorious in the suit, he was also awarded attorney's fees.

ON DECEMBER 12, 1899, GEORGE GRANT
RECEIVED PATENT NUMBER 638,920
FOR HIS RATHER SIMPLE BUT
GAME-CHANGING IDEA—THE GOLF TEE.

ATTRACTED TO HORSEHIDE

For a fan, catching a ball in a major league game is a big deal, but catching two is almost unheard of, especially if you didn't see them coming. On August 17, 1957, Phillies outfielder Richie Ashburn was at bat and hit a screaming liner into the stands that smacked Alice Roth in the head. Attendants ran to her aid and, although she didn't seem badly hurt, the game was temporarily halted while a stretcher team came to take Ms. Roth for medical attention. Once she was secured, the game continued and, again, Ashburn slammed a screamer into the stands, striking Ms. Roth as she lay strapped in the stretcher.

• •

Reuters reported on July 18, 2007, that officials at the Masters games in Milan, Italy, realizing that the invited athletes ranged in age from thirty-five all the way to their nineties, announced that the javelin competition would be relocated to an area farther away from the other planned events.

• •

WHAT A REAL MOTHER

The Los Angeles television station KLAC reported on May 11, 2006, that a man filed a sex- and age-discrimination lawsuit against the Los Angeles Angels baseball team for $4,000. He claimed the team wouldn't give him a free red nylon tote bag during a 2005 Mother's Day promotion because he wasn't a woman over eighteen. Los Angeles psychologist Michael Cohn alleged that thousands of males and fans under age eighteen were each entitled to $4,000 in damages. The Angels announced that, at their next promotion, they would give the bags to anyone over the age of eighteen. They were soon notified that if they did that, they would then be violating the rights of people under age eighteen.

* * *

On April 29, 2007, CNN reported on the annual "crying sumo" events that are held in various Japanese cities. The story explained that traditional sumo wrestlers hold elaborately dressed toddlers in front of them during the events and do whatever is necessary to make the children cry.

* * *

TRICK PLAY

The Carlisle Indians had a special play up their sleeve and decided there was no better time to try it out than during their October 31, 1903, game against the Harvard Crimson. On the game's opening kickoff, Carlisle player Jimmie Johnson was in place to receive, and his teammates closed in around him. Johnson stashed the ball inside the jersey of teammate Charlie Dillon, and the rest of the Carlisle players quickly pulled off their leather helmets and hugged them to their chests as if they were footballs. The entire team headed upfield toward Harvard's goal line. The Crimson were confused and had no idea who actually had the ball or even where the ball was. Dillon, the only player still wearing his helmet and the only one ignored by the Harvard team, trotted down the length of the field and scored a touchdown.

"It wasn't my arm [that was injured]. It was my forearm."

—St. Louis Cardinals pitcher Joaquin Andujar,
The Associated Press, 1988

EXCUSES, EXCUSES, EXCUSES

Athletes can be just as imaginative in finding excuses to get out of playing as they are during the game. For example:

Third baseman Wade Boggs once injured his back while putting on a pair of cowboy boots.

Infielder José Cardenal of the Chicago Cubs missed a game claiming he had been kept awake all night by the sound of crickets chirping.

Outfielder Ken Griffey, Jr., missed one game in 1994 due to a groin injury sustained when his protective cup pinched one of his testicles.

Left fielder Kevin Mitchell of the New York Mets strained a muscle while vomiting. He also broke a tooth on a frozen chocolate doughnut, which had been left in the microwave too long and hardened. It was the doughnut incident that led to a root canal, and he was later fitted with a gold tooth as a replacement.

ARRESTING PLAY

Defenseman Frank Beaton of the World Hockey Association's Birmingham Bulls was battling it out with the Cincinnati Stingers on February 19, 1978, when he got a severe penalty—he was arrested. After the first period, Beaton was taken into custody by six police officers and arrested for an assault he had committed two years previously on a gas station attendant. According to police records, the attendant accidentally spilled gasoline on Beaton's Corvette, and Beaton went crazy and broke the man's cheekbone.

. . . .

"Somehow, the ear must have gotten into Vaeno's mouth, and the pulling motion of that opposing player resulted in it coming off."
—Attorney for rugby player Latu Vaeno, explaining to the jury why his client wasn't guilty of assault. On November 2, 1987, Vaeno was sentenced to six months in jail.

. . . .

ARE THE VOICES IN MY HEAD BOTHERING YOU?

Despite his criminal record, which includes raping the family babysitter (for which he was sentenced to four years in prison), his failure to pay income tax, theft, and misdemeanor assault, former world heavyweight boxing champion (and last man to fight Muhammad Ali) Trevor Berbick won his deportation hearing in Toronto in December 2000 and was allowed to stay in Canada for at least five years. During the hearing, Berbick defended his criminal record by stating that it was the result of a conspiracy masterminded by boxer Larry Holmes, and his title loss to Mike Tyson only happened because someone pumped gas into his hotel room the night before the fight. His bizarre testimony took a turn for the weirder when he suddenly yelled out, "Power nap!" and immediately fell asleep. However, his troubles were far from over, and when he was caught in the United States in 2002, he was deported back to his native Jamaica. Four years later on October 28, 2006, Berbick was attacked at a church in Norwich, Jamaica, by two men who beat him to death with a steel pipe. One of the assailants was his twenty-year-old nephew, Harold Berbick, who was sentenced to life in prison.

A HOP, SKIP, AND A JUMP

It had to be the most memorable game in the history of baseball. On May 23, 1883, the Snorkeys of Philadelphia destroyed the Hoppers 34–11. What made the game so fascinating is that all the players for the Snorkeys had only one arm. And the Hoppers consisted entirely of men who had lost one of their legs. It's even more curious that every player on both teams was an employee of the Reading Railroad who had lost a limb in a work-related accident, except one Civil War veteran who had lost an arm at the Battle of Gettysburg.

"The only rule I got is if you slide, get up."

—Boston Red Sox pitcher Bill "Spaceman" Lee,
USA Today, October 25, 1989

In order to save the price of admission, hundreds of fans climbed to the roof of the Pacific Glass Works Factory in San Francisco to watch the November 29, 1900, Stanford–California football game. The roof couldn't handle the extra weight and collapsed, causing the death of thirteen fans who fell into vats of molten glass.

A SHOT IN THE ARM

We've heard of a boxer taking one on the chin, but in July 2001, thirty-eight-year-old Tony Ayala, Jr., took one in the shoulder. He was shot in the shoulder by a woman whose house he had broken into with the intent to commit a sexual assault in December 2000. Ayala was still under court-ordered monitoring but was allowed to fight that night. This wasn't the boxer's first run-in with attempts below the belt. Ayala had a promising career in 1983 (27–0, 24 knockouts), but it was cut short by a rape conviction for which he served sixteen years in prison. According to a September 18, 2001, article in the *New York Times*, Ayala won the ten-round July fight with a decision—all the while wearing a court-ordered ankle bracelet.

ALL-TIME BLOOPER REEL FAVORITE

On May 26, 1993, during a Texas Rangers versus Cleveland Indians game, Carlos Martínez hit a fly ball that Rangers center fielder José Canseco lost sight of as he crossed the warning track. The ball bounced off of Canseco's head and over the wall for a home run. The television show *This Week in Baseball* awarded it the best blooper in its twenty-one years of broadcasting. Obviously impressed with Canseco's heading skills, the Harrisburg Heat, a professional indoor soccer team, offered him a contract, but he turned them down.

. . . .

Canseco's amazing blooper was only made possible by the fact that on August 31, 1992, in the middle of a game and while he was in the on-deck circle, the Oakland Athletics traded Canseco to the Texas Rangers for Rubén Sierra, Jeff Russell, and Bobby Witt.

. . . .

THERE'S ONE BORN
EVERY MINUTE

On August 26, 1890, New Yorker Sylvester F. Wilson, (a.k.a. W. S. Franklin) announced the formation of the Young Ladies Baseball Club #1 by placing help-wanted advertisements around the city. Knowing that skill alone wouldn't fill the stands, Franklin noted that all applicants "must be young, not over twenty, good looking with a good figure." Franklin's team of buxom baseball beauties raised more than eyebrows as they toured the country taking on various men's teams. There was, however, some concern that the "women" had a few more balls than bats, and their team photograph showed some very manly looking women. Some of the team members' names such as Effie Earl, May Howard, and Annie Grant might even have been a little tongue-in-cheek.

Georgia Tech's famous 222-0 hammering of Cumberland College on October 7, 1916, is generally recognized as football's worst beating. But on November 16, 1927, Haven High of Haven, Kansas, destroyed local rival Sylvia High 256-0.

A GAME OF WITS

The Ojibwe, or Chippewa, tribe resented the harsh, oppressive policies of the British and their occupation of Fort Michilimackinac, a Native American stronghold in Michigan located on the southern shore of the Straits of Mackinac connecting Lake Huron and Lake Michigan. On June 2, 1763, as part of the larger movement known as Pontiac's Rebellion, a group of Ojibwe began playing a game of *baaga'adowe* (a forerunner of modern lacrosse) outside the fort. The British soldiers enjoyed watching the game and were soon enthralled with the action and let down their guard. When the ball was "accidentally" knocked over the fort walls, the players all rushed after it and, as planned, attacked and killed a large number of the complacent soldiers and residents. The Ojibwe held the fort for a year before the British reoccupied it under the condition of providing the Native Americans with better and more abundant gifts.

. . . .

"Anybody's best pitch is the one the batters ain't hitting that day."

—New York Giants/Cincinnati Reds pitcher
Christy "Big Six" Mathewson, *Sporting News*,
August 6, 1948

. . . .

SAY IT AIN'T SO

Anyone who watched the 1988 film *Bull Durham* heard that minor league baseball players traditionally referred to the majors as "The Show." But Bob Halloran, an ESPN analyst, did some research on the subject and came to the conclusion that the filmmakers simply made up the term. No one, he claimed, had ever used the term or had even heard of it before the movie. He admitted, however, that Arkansas Travelers owner Bert Parke said some minor leaguers refer to the majors as "The Big Club."

The legendary Yogi Berra was asked to make a few opening remarks to kick off the festivities on Yogi Berra Night in his hometown of St. Louis at Sportsmen's Park. Berra stepped up to the microphone on August 26, 1947, and uttered the famous line, "I want to thank everyone for making this night necessary."

LEST WE FORGET

Before the start of a September 15, 2001, Pop Warner football league game (kids age thirteen and fourteen) in Milford, Massachusetts, both teams conducted a brief memorial observance for the victims of the September 11, 2001, terrorist attacks. According to a September 18, 2001, article in the *Milford Daily News*, even though the observance was prearranged, the referee nonetheless threw a yellow penalty flag, penalizing the home team fifteen yards for delaying the start of the game. The referee wouldn't back down on the penalty, even after protests broke out.

"Well, that kind of puts a damper on even a Yankees win."

—Announcer Phil "The Scooter" Rizzuto, explaining his reaction to the news that Pope Paul VI had died on August 6, 1978

RING OF DEATH

It was a tragedy both inside and outside of the ring when Ray "Boom Boom" Mancini retained his World Boxing Association lightweight title with a fourteenth round technical knockout over South Korean Duk Koo Kim. Mancini unleashed a barrage of thirty-nine straight punches during the thirteenth round of the November 13, 1982, fight at Caesars Palace. Just nineteen seconds into the fourteenth, Mancini clobbered Kim with two enormous rights, and the Korean dropped to the canvas. Kim was carried out of the ring. He dropped into a coma and died four days later without regaining consciousness. Kim's mother, Sun-Nyo, distraught over the loss of her son, committed suicide by drinking a bottle of pesticide two and a half months later. Another related death was that of Richard Green, who refereed the match. He committed suicide on July 1, 1983, after refereeing only one additional bout.

· ·

If the deaths involved in the Mancini–Kim boxing match weren't bad enough, some six years later, while preparing features about the Summer Olympics in Seoul, South Korea, NBC discovered that Kim's son (an infant at the time of his father's death) had never been told what happened to his dad. He believed his father was alive and still boxing professionally in America.

· ·

181

IF YOU GOT IT, FLAUNT IT!

The French news agency Agence France-Presse reported on October 23, 2001, that a judge in Rio de Janeiro rejected a defamation lawsuit against a biographer brought by the daughters of deceased Brazilian soccer player Manuel Francisco dos Santos (known by his nickname "Garrincha," which means "little bird"). The daughters objected to the biographer's reference to Garrincha as a sex machine with a penis nearly ten inches long. The girls thought the disclosure was an insult to the memory of their father, who died in an alcoholic coma of cirrhosis of the liver on January 19, 1983, but Judge Joao Wehbi Dib concluded that most Brazilian men would view Garrincha's purported measurement and sexual prowess with admiration.

A WHIRLING DERVISH

It turned into a box-a-thon when light-heavyweight British-born Bobby Frankham went ballistic on nearly everyone in the ring. In December 1987, he was fighting Billy Sims at Wembley Arena when referee Richie Davis stopped him. Frankham let Davis know he didn't agree with Davis's decision with a right punch. He pounded the referee in the face twice before turning his attention to Sims's corner men, and then he had a go at Sims himself. Then it was time for the rival fans to get involved, and the referee needed a police escort to accompany him from the ring. The British Boxing Board of Control called Frankham's actions an utterly disgraceful episode, to which Frankham commented, "I just had a brainstorm," adding that it was "a bad way to get famous." The board banned Frankham from professional boxing for life.

A REAL HATCHET JOB

Former pro football punter Chris Hanson played only one-third of the 2003 season with the Jacksonville Jaguars because of an accidental self-inflicted leg injury. Jaguars coach Jack Del Rio placed a tree stump and an ax in the Jaguars' locker room as a symbolic reminder of his theme encouraging players to "keep choppin' wood." According to an October 11, 2003, article in the *Washington Post*, several players hacked away at the stump, but when Hanson got his hands on the ax handle it was a swing and a miss. He wound up seriously damaging his nonkicking foot and was put on the injured reserve list.

• •

Even Nostradamus didn't see this one coming. San Francisco manager Alvin Dark joked about the lousy hitting skills of his star pitcher, Gaylord Perry, saying, "A man'll walk on the moon before Gaylord hits a homer." On July 20, 1969, Neil Armstrong was the first man to set foot on the moon, and thirty-four-minutes after this historic event, Perry knocked out his first major league round-tripper.

• •

DON'T BE SO GAY!

Cornerback Randall "Blue" Gay and the New England Patriots won Super Bowl XXXIX against the Philadelphia Eagles in 2005. One of Gay's former college professors tried to order a replica jersey but was turned down. The National Football League's official online merchandiser, NFLshop.com, refused to print "Gay" on the back of a Patriots jersey because it was one of the 1,159 blacklisted words deemed offensive or related to drugs, sex, or gangs. The *San Francisco Chronicle* reported on April 3, 2005, that two weeks after the story was released, the word "Gay" was removed from the list because it was actually the name of a player.

• •

American inventor Thomas Alva Edison is known for creating a lot of firsts, the light bulb and the phonograph, to name two. But did you know that he also produced the first sporting film? On June 14, 1894, in his laboratory in West Orange, New Jersey, Edison made the first-ever filmed boxing match—an exhibition between Jack Cushing and Mike Leonard.

• •

GRIN AND BEAR IT

"Rugby player spent months with foe's tooth in his forehead"
read the *USA Today* headline from July 17, 2007. Twenty-four-
year-old Australian rugby league player Ben Czislowski of
Brisbane's team Wynnum violently collided with Matt Austin
of the Tweed Heads on April 1, 2007, and was left with a head
wound that required stitches. Soon Czislowski complained of
shooting pains in his head and an eye infection, and doctors
told him the cause of his discomfort was a tooth. But it wasn't
his tooth, it was one of Austin's. Czislowki told reporters that if
"[Austin] wants it back, he can have it." Austin might actually
have wanted the tooth back because he lost several others in his
collision with Czislowski.

MOVING VIOLATION

Cleveland Browns fan Mike Meredith and a couple of his buddies converted a riding mower into a mobile couch in 2005 to cruise between tailgate parties because, "I was wasting time walking around when I could be sitting here eating hot dogs and drinking beer." He usually drove the "Go-Kouch" around the Municipal Parking Lot, but he claimed that on November 23, 2008, police officers waved him through and allowed him to drive on the street toward the stadium. Soon, another officer, who didn't find the humor in the situation, ticketed him for driving an unregistered vehicle and having expired plates. Meredith said that tailgaters pooled $500 to pay his tickets, but according to the *Plain Dealer* on December 14, 2008, he decided to fight the charges and donate the money to the Make-a-Wish Foundation.

A RACE TO THE FINISH

May 30, 1912, marked the second Indianapolis 500, and Ralph Mulford, who many believe was cheated out of first place in the first Indy 500, had considerable mechanical trouble. He was considering not finishing the race, but officials told him and his pit crew that if he didn't pass the finish line he wouldn't be eligible for tenth-place prize money. What they didn't tell Mulford was that he had to hurry. Mulford didn't want to strain his car any more than he had to, so he took his time finishing the race. He and his riding mechanic even stopped once for an order of fried chicken and ice cream, and it was even reported that the team changed shock absorbers for a gentler ride. Mulford finally finished the race and drove through deserted grandstands as the sun was beginning to set. He crossed the finish line after eight hours and fifty-three minutes, averaging 56.285 miles per hour—a time that is still in the record books as the slowest finishing speed in the history of the Indianapolis 500.

DOWN FROM THE ROCKY TOP

The year was 1908, and the Tennessee Volunteers were in a heap of trouble with Georgia on their own two-yard line. They needed a miracle, and they got it in the form of a whiskey-drinking, heavily whiskered man toting a .38 revolver. The man stormed onto the field with blood in his eyes (probably more like bloodshot eyes) and staggered over to the Georgia team. With potently vaporous breath, he threatened, "First man who crosses the goal line gets a bullet in his carcass." Police arrived and whisked the whiskey-soaked intruder out of the October 24 game, but his threat still hung in the air (as did his breath). Georgia fumbled the ball on the very next play and was never able to score for the rest of the game. Tennessee won 10–0.

. . . .

University of Illinois pole-vaulter Lane Lohr made the approach and cleared the crossbar during an attempt on June 5, 1985. But there's a hitch: The pole fell forward and underneath him and caught short. The force of Lohr's falling body ripped his pants completely off. The pole-vaulter vaulted for cover.

. . . .

OH, FIDDLESTICKS!

Dave "The Dragon" Lockwood has become the head of a dynasty in a little-appreciated sport—tiddlywinks. Lockwood, of Silver Spring, Maryland, wants his five children (Sam[antha], Alex[andra], Max[imilian], Jon[athan], and Ben[jamin]) to become the winningest winkers in the world. Having learned to love the game as a student at MIT, in 2001, Dave was ranked number one by the English Tiddlywinks Association. According to a January 21, 2006, article in the *Washington Post*, Dave was hoping to persuade Prince Philip, reportedly a serious winker himself, to recommend that tiddlywinks be chosen as a demonstration sport during the 2012 Summer Olympic Games in London. If the Games can have synchronized swimming, he said with a wink and a smile, why can't there be winks? In case you missed the 2012 Olympics, Dave's dream didn't come true.

A HOLE FOR ONE

Seventy-seven-year-old Jimmy Hogg and four of his friends were just teeing off from the first hole at his Fife, Scotland, golf club in 1996 when Hogg suffered a major heart attack and died. Out of respect for the game, Hogg's partners waited somberly for the ambulance to come and take their dear departed friend away, and then they resumed their game and played on. "I'm sure Jimmy would have wanted us to do that," said one. "He would have done the same."

· ·

Here's a different twist on sports and the color barrier. On May 16, 1955, Rocky Marciano successfully defended his heavyweight title for the fifth time, defeating challenger Don Cockell in the ninth round of their bout in San Francisco. This was the last all-white fight for the heavyweight crown.

· ·

BETTER THAN A SHARP STICK IN THE EYE

Poor Daniel Caruso thought he would psych himself up before his bout for the Golden Gloves Tournament of Champions in New York in January 1992 by punching himself in the face. He had seen former champion Marvin Hagler do the same warm-up routine and thought he would emulate Hagler. We'll never know if it was nerves or whether he just got caught up in the moment, but Caruso punched himself so hard he broke his own nose. Doctors examined the self-defeated boxer and declared he wasn't fit to fight—Caruso was disqualified.

· ·

Jack Norworth and Albert von Tilzer—the men who wrote and composed the 1908 anthem to baseball, "Take Me Out to the Ballgame"— had never been to a baseball game.

· ·

BEST OF THE BEST

When you ask a baseball fan who was the greatest hitter in the sport, you'll usually hear names like Babe Ruth, Ty Cobb, Mickey Mantle, Barry Bonds, Hank Aaron, Lou Gehrig, John Paciorek . . . wait a minute, who? His name was John Paciorek, and he was a Houston rookie outfielder. On September 29, 1963, this eighteen-year-old began and ended his major league career. Paciorek singled three times, walked twice, scored four runs, and drove in three runs. He finished the season with a 1.000 batting average. After injuring his back, Paciorek never appeared in another major league game. But he ended his career as baseball's most "perfect hitter."

. . . .

"Man arraigned on charge of assault with bowling ball"

—*Buffalo News* headline, March 16, 2012

. . . .

STOP PULLING
MY TAIL

It's called *coleo,* and it is a traditional Venezuelan and Colombian sport, similar to a rodeo and less bloody than bullfighting. The sport involves four men on horseback chasing cattle at high speeds through a narrow pathway called a *manga de coleo* with the objective of tipping them over. They do this by grabbing the calf or bull by the tail and yanking on it until the animal falls over, and whoever does this the most times wins. A spokesman for the national *coleo* organization told the *New York Times* on September 10, 2006, that *coleo* is "truly Venezuelan."

• •

A delusional fifty-six-year-old Emanuel Kuvakos was arrested on charges of sending threatening e-mails to two Chicago sports team executives. Kuvakos accused the men of stealing his ideas for winning championships and promised to seek revenge on them. According to an April 18, 2012, article in the *Chicago Tribune*, one of the victims was a former general manager of the Chicago Cubs, who haven't won a World Series since 1908.

• •

194

THE GAME OF NAMES

Baseball Teams from the International League (1884–Present)

1891–1905, PROVIDENCE CLAMDIGGERS

1919, READING COAL BARONS

1885, ROCHESTER FLOUR CITIES

1891–1892, ROCHESTER HOP BITTERS

1912–1920, ROCHESTER HUSTLERS

1888–1889, ROCHESTER JINGOES

1895, SCRANTON COAL HEAVERS

· ·

In 1993, the career of New Jersey Devils mascot Slapshot the Puck came to an end after he was sued for improperly touching three women.

· ·

DON'T TOUCH THAT DIAL

It is referred to as the Heidi Game or Heidi Bowl, and it is considered to be one of the biggest blunders in network television history. On November 17, 1968, Joe Namath and the New York Jets were leading the Oakland Raiders 32–29 with only sixty-five seconds left. The game had already run long, and thinking it was a done deal, NBC decided to pull the plug on the game and go to their scheduled program, the made-for-TV film *Heidi*. What made the decision so memorable was that while the audience was watching *Heidi*, Daryle "The Mad Bomber" Lamonica rallied the Raiders to a pair of touchdowns in the final minute of the game to produce an incredible 43–32 upset, which was never seen nationally.

PUT A SOCK IN IT

An unnamed forty-one-year-old engineer living in suburban Toronto has amassed a very unique sports memorabilia collection—socks. Interviewed in a lengthy profile in the November 11, 2006, edition of the *National Post*, the man admitted to collecting and wearing approximately eight-hundred pairs of sports socks over a fifteen-year period. More than half of the socks are from professional athletes. The man does not consider himself a fetishist; rather, he is a custodian of history (even though he admitted keeping the collection a secret from his wife).

. . . .

Franklin Delano Roosevelt may be the only four-term president and one of the most beloved presidents of all time, but he sure couldn't pitch. On April 16, 1940, Opening Day in Washington, D.C.'s Griffith Stadium, the president wound up and threw the first ball of the season, and it was a direct hit—right into the camera lens of *Washington Post* photographer Irving Schlossenberg.

. . . .

STILL BETTER THAN BEING A CUBS FAN

A lot of students endure some form of harassment in high school, but Joshua Vannoy was so humiliated that he and his family felt they had to move. During the 2006 football playoff game between the Denver Broncos and the Pittsburgh Steelers, Joshua decided to wear a Broncos jersey to his school, Beaver Falls High School, located near Pittsburgh. According to a January 17, 2007, article in the *Pittsburgh Post-Gazette*, one of Joshua's teachers was so incensed at the eighteen-year-old's choice of clothing that he made Joshua sit on the floor and allowed other students to throw wads of paper at him. Because he was, in the words of the teacher, a "stinking Denver fan." The following January after the incident, the Vannoys moved, and Joshua and his parents filed a lawsuit against the Big Beaver Falls Area School District.

GOING FOR BROKE

It was a win and a loss on the same night. Thailand's World Boxing Council flyweight champ Sot Chitalada knocked out challenger Charlie Magri of Great Britain, successfully defending his title and raising his record to 22–2–1. A celebration broke out in Chitalada's camp, and there was much dancing, hugging, and laughing. But suddenly Chitalada realized something was missing—his wallet. Apparently, a pickpocket had wormed his way into the celebration and took off with Chitalada's wallet with a check for $104,000, his winnings from the bout.

The Phillie Phanatic has spent nearly as much time in the courtroom as he has on the field:

At a church carnival in 1995, the Phanatic was found guilty of knocking a seventy-two-year-old man to the ground by slamming him with his belly. A jury awarded the injured man $100,000.

One year later, the Phanatic was sued by a pregnant woman who he kicked in the stomach, and she was awarded $25,000.

The Phanatic was also sued by a man who accused him of jumping onto his lap, and he was awarded an unspecified amount of money. The man claimed the force of the impact on his nether region made him impotent. "We lost some money there," the Phanatic explained to the *Philadelphia Inquirer*.

LADIES FIRST

Sylvester F. Wilson, who started several female baseball clubs, including the Chicago Blackstockings and the Young Ladies Baseball Club #1, was described in the press as "a female baseball manager, ticket scalper, all around swindler, and professional debaucher of female morals." In October 1891, he was sentenced to five years in Sing Sing prison for abducting Libbie Sutherland, who played on one of his female clubs. The *Kansas City Star* commented on Wilson, stating, "He has been arrested more than 100 times and for various crimes, and Secretary Jenkins of the New York Society for the Prevention of Cruelty to Children says he has ruined more young girls than any man living."

A HUSH FELL OVER THE CROWD

The El Paso Diablos, a Double A team, were completely silenced at the end of the fifth. What happened was that plate umpire Brian Owens made a questionable call that went against the Diablos and the fans reacted wildly. Stadium announcer Paul Strelzin cranked up Linda Ronstadt's version of "When Will I Be Loved" over the PA (lyrics include "I've been cheated/ Been mistreated/ When will I be loved?"). The ump didn't appreciate the slam and signaled for Strelzin to stop the music. However, at the end of the inning, Strelzin, still stinging from the bad call and probably offended at being censored, began playing the song again. This time, Owens ordered him to leave the stadium, and for the remainder of the May 24, 1988, game, no batters were introduced, no music was played, and no announcements were made.

THE BLAME GAME

On April 29, 2007, St. Louis Cardinals pitcher Josh Hancock was killed in a car crash after he collided with a flatbed tow truck that was stopped in the left lane assisting another vehicle that had been involved in a previous wreck. According to a May 25, 2007, article in the *Houston Chronicle*, Hancock's accident took place after midnight on Interstate 64, and a police report indicated that Hancock was intoxicated, speeding, not wearing a seat belt, and talking on his cell phone. Nonetheless, one month after the accident, Hancock's father filed a lawsuit blaming everyone but his son; he sued the tow truck company, the tow truck operator, the driver being assisted by the tow truck operator, and the restaurant where Hancock had been drinking.

203

On April 9, 1945, the National Football League decreed that henceforth all players must wear socks during the games.

A REAL DIE-HARD FAN

Paul "Buddy" Wellener was a lifelong fan of the Pittsburgh Steelers and a dedicated season ticket holder for forty-two years. When Wellener died unexpectedly on March 12, 2000, his family wanted to make his final resting place feel more like home. So they bought and installed over his grave two blue plastic seats from Three Rivers Stadium. At Three Rivers, the Welleners had six seats numbered 3 through 8, and they were able to buy three pairs of seats with the same numbers for $2,100. According to a January 7, 2001, article in the *Pittsburgh Post-Gazette*, one pair was to go on Wellener's grave in the Mt. Lebanon Cemetery and the other two pairs were to be given to his two sons.

UP, UP, AND AWAY

The rough-and-tumble early days of football were also the most inventive years of the sport. Take, for example, the November 24, 1904, game between the Tennessee Volunteers and Alabama. Fullback Sam McAllester wore a specially designed leather belt equipped with large loops on each side. On a fifty-yard touchdown drive, McAllester was repeatedly lifted by the loops by his two halfbacks and literally thrown over the top of the line. They used the technique as they approached Alabama's end zone and launched McAllester to the only score of the game, giving the Vols a 7–0 victory through air power.

· ·

At a track meet in Rome on April 3, 1981, Canadian high jumper Arnie Boldt cleared 6 feet 8½ inches. Even though that was nearly a foot below the world record at that time, it's awesome when you consider that Boldt only has one leg.

· ·

THE KISS OF DEATH

The Cincinnati Reds were playing a home game against the St. Louis Cardinals at Great American Ball Park on May 7, 2003, but the real action was in the bleachers. When the Kiss Cam panned the crowd, David Horton gave his girl a smooch, and the entire stadium was watching—especially Horton's parole officer, who was also in the crowd. "Out of all the coincidences, we had twenty or thirty thousand people at the ballpark, and who do they put on the Kiss Cam? And then, who is there but his parole officer?" said Richard Goldberg, Horton's attorney. According to a June 10, 2003, article in the *Cincinnati Enquirer*, Horton had been indicted for trafficking and possession of cocaine and failed to appear in court. His parole officer and a police officer arrested him on the spot and removed him from his front-row seat. He was sentenced to four and a half years in prison.

THE MAN BEHIND THE MASK

The mascot's name is Paisley Panda, and he entertains the crowds during St. Mirren Football (soccer) Club games in England. Mascots are usually just funny distractions during a game, but Paisley Panda's antics got out of control and he was fired (actually, the guy wearing the suit was fired). According to an October 5, 2003, report from the BBC, police and the team's management had warned twenty-four-year-old Chris Kelso, who was performing inside the panda suit, about his on-field behavior. But after he used a rival club's jersey as toilet paper he was promptly fired. Kelso had been warned during the previous season for making inappropriate gestures with an inflatable sheep.

GOING OFF
HALF-COCKED

The *Birmingham News* on September 30, 2003, reported the case of an enraged Alabama college football fan who did more than shoot his mouth off. Forty-six-year-old Joseph Logan of Pinson, Alabama, was arrested for assault shortly after his beloved Crimson Tide lost to the rival Arkansas Razorbacks by a score of 34–31. Logan began slamming doors, screaming around the house, and smashing dishes into the sink. Logan's twenty-year-old son, Seth, foolishly chose this time to ask his father if he could help Seth buy a car, and Logan responded by grabbing a gun and putting Seth into a headlock. Logan's blood pressure was probably a coursing Crimson Tide, and he fired a bullet near Seth's ear. A sheriff's deputy responded to Logan's actions by saying, "I know we take football serious in the South, but that's crossing the line."

FEMME FATALE

The first organized boxing match between women took place on March 16, 1876, between Nelly Saunders and Rose Harland. They started throwing leather, and four action-packed rounds later, officials at the Hill's Theatre in New York gave a narrow decision to Saunders. Not only did the winner receive $200 but she also was awarded something a little less politically correct—a silver-plated butter dish.

· ·

On March 22, 1893, Smith College in Northampton, Massachusetts, became the first school to play competitive women's basketball. Sounds like a huge boon for women's rights, but not for men—no men were allowed to watch.

· ·

A REAL POP FLY

Hoyt Wilhelm, the Orioles' thirty-six-year-old knuckleballer, was at the mound and facing off with the White Sox in Chicago's Comiskey Park when thousands of late arrivals swarmed into the stadium and clouded his view. "I never seen nothin' like them. I couldn't pitch through them," Wilhelm said. He was talking about millions of gnats that were suddenly attracted to the field. There was a six-minute delay of the game while the grounds crew tried to fumigate the park, but to no avail. Then someone had a bright idea—fireworks. Dozens of smoke bombs were attached to the fireworks that were intended for the finale of the June 2, 1959, game. Desperate times call for desperate measures. The smoke bombs worked, but the biggest pest, according to the Sox, was Wilhelm himself. He won his eighth straight game over two seasons and bombed the Sox 3–2.

. . . .

**"It is dangerous for an athlete to believe
his own publicity, good or bad."**

—Bob Uecker, *Catcher in the Wry*, by Bob Uecker
(G. P. Putnam's Sons, New York, 1982)

. . . .

TRADE YA

From the 1950s to the 1960s, Harry Chiti, father of major league coach Dom Chiti, was a Major League Baseball catcher who played for the Chicago Cubs, Kansas City Athletics, Detroit Tigers, and New York Mets. In his last year, Chiti was a part of transactions between the A's and the Cleveland Indians, but on April 25, 1962, before he even got out on the field for the Indians, he was acquired by the New York Mets for "a player to be named later." However, on June 15, 1962, after an unimpressive fifteen games and a batting average of only .195, Chiti was sent back to the Indians. Therefore, according to the contractual agreement, when Chiti was accepted back by the Indians, that made him "the player to be named later." This made Harry Chiti the first player in the history of Major League Baseball to be traded for himself.

. . . .

The only player to be traded for himself since then was John McDonald of the Toronto Blue Jays. He was traded to the Detroit Tigers on July 22, 2005. On November 10, 2005, McDonald was sent back to Toronto in exchange for monetary considerations. Therefore, he was essentially traded for himself.

. . . .

A DOG'S LIFE

Like a donkey being led with a carrot, greyhounds are led around a track by those pesky mechanical rabbits they never can catch. But on February 19, 1978, during the fifth race at the Hollywood (Florida) Greyhound Track, a nearly two-year-old long shot named Lucky Maury had devised a plan. As the gates flew open, the dog took two jumps down the track, made a U-turn, eluding a frantic patrol judge who tried to grab him, and bolted in the opposite direction, intending to catch the rabbit as it rounded the bend. He met the rascally rabbit head-on at the clubhouse turn and was soon joined by all the other greyhounds in a hilarious free-for-all. Fans had wagered $47,000 on the race, and all bets were refunded.

· ·

"The biggest thrill a ballplayer can have is when your son takes after you. That happened when my Bobby was in his championship Little League game. He really showed me something. Struck out three times. Made an error that lost the game. Parents were throwing things at our car and swearing at us as we drove off. Gosh, I was proud."

—Bob Uecker, *Sports Illustrated*,
September 8, 1980

· ·

SCALPING THEMSELVES

Three hapless ticket scalpers in their twenties were arrested in St. Petersburg, Florida, on what is probably the worst scheme in scamming history. Calvin Calhoun, Lavance Palmer, and Kelvin Charles used a stolen credit card to purchase 180 Tampa Bay Devil Rays baseball tickets for a weekend series against the Seattle Mariners. According to a July 13, 2002, article in the *Tampa Tribune*, the three scalpers intended to resell the tickets at a profit without taking into consideration that the attendance at Devil Rays games was among the lowest in the major leagues. In fact, there were 127,000 empty seats for the four games—well, actually 127,003, because the scalpers were arrested and were unable to attend the games.

RICOCHET RABBIT

We've all heard the expression "That's using your head," but
Washington Senators pitcher Ed Linke took the phrase literally.
On July 26, 1935, Linke threw a screamer at Yankee Jesse Hill,
who cracked a liner right back at Linke, smacking him squarely
on the forehead. The ball bounced off Linke's skull and ricocheted
into catcher Jack Redmond's mitt. Redmond grabbed the ball and
fired it to second base, catching a confused Yankee runner off the
bag and completing an inning-ending double play.

· ·

**On February 26, 1941, referee Clarence Rosen stopped
a brutal and bloody fight between Pat Carroll and
Sammy Secreet, declaring both fighters were too
battered to continue. He ruled the fight a double
technical knockout—the rarest call in the sport.**

· ·

AH, HE'S YELLOW

Most people know that Jackie Robinson broke through the color barrier in Major League Baseball when he debuted with the Brooklyn Dodgers in 1947. But the era of baseball as an all-white game actually ended on August 2, 1938, and it still happened because of the Dodgers. General manager Larry MacPhail wanted to experiment during a game with St. Louis with a special dandelion yellow baseball instead of the traditional white one. The ball was used in game one of a doubleheader, and Johnny Mize is credited with being the only major leaguer to hit a yellow homer. Players and fans all liked the yellow ball since it was easier to see, but in game two, the teams went back to the standard white ball, and the yellow hide was retired forever.

. . . .

"I like my players to be married and in debt. That's the way you motivate them."

—Major League Baseball Hall of Famer Ernie Banks,
New York Times, April 11, 1976

. . . .

HOCKEY REVIEW

Twenty-four-year-old Bryan Allison was treated and released from a hospital in Buffalo, New York, after falling twenty feet to the ground while attempting to throw his television off a second-floor balcony. According to a November 19, 2001, article in the *Buffalo News*, Allison became enraged after he and his brother watched his team lose in a videotape of a 1989 National Hockey League playoff game. He grabbed the television and attempted to chuck it off the balcony. Unfortunately, he forgot to let go in time, and he went over with the set.

. . . .

February 20, 1944, marks the date of what could easily be the dullest game in hockey history. It looked more like a skating competition than hockey as Toronto and Chicago tied in a scoreless competition. There were no penalties called, either, which made the game not only boring, but also one of a kind.

. . . .

During a game on May 4, 1999, a disgruntled fan pushed the Baltimore Orioles mascot, Oriole Bird, off his perch on the right-field bleachers. This bird couldn't fly, so it plummeted ten feet, breaking his ankle and forcing the man in the bird suit to spend the next forty days in a wheelchair. He sued and managed to collect $59,000 from the fan.

SPORTS SNOOZER

n most hockey seasons there are usually final scores of 1–0, and here might be a dozen or more baseball games with that score— ut basketball? It happened in central Illinois on March 6, 1930, etween Georgetown High School and Homer High. The Homer enter fouled a guard in the first period, and Georgetown got on he board early with a foul shot. But the Homer underdogs had a lan to stall until the last minute and then do a full-court press. eorgetown appreciated Homer's effort and simply allowed the eam to hold the ball. With only three minutes left to play, Homer nissed a final shot but was fouled. Their plan was working. Jnfortunately, the two free throws failed, and Georgetown won he game 1–0 in what will forever remain basketball's lowest-scoring game.

"I like being close [after he moved his locker] to the bats."

—Don Mattingly, *Major League Baseball Newsletter*, September 198⁹

BLOWING A WHISTLE ON THEMSELVES

Coaches are notorious for warning players not to engage in horseplay, especially in the locker room. But that rule doesn't always apply to coaches themselves. A January 15, 2009, article in the *Pittsburgh Post-Gazette* reported on two assistant football coaches from Westminster College in New Wilmington, Pennsylvania—Scott Coy and Darren DeMeio—who were in Nashville, Tennessee, for a coaches' convention. The two men, with a combined weight of 525 pounds, were wrestling in their hotel at four in the morning when they accidentally smashed through the double-paned window in their fourth-floor room and crashed to the ground in their underwear.

THE LATE WINNER

Some of the earliest Olympic events make synchronized swimming look about as sissified as, well, synchronized swimming. One such event was called pancration, a mixture of boxing, wrestling, and endurance that had virtually no rules. During the pancration event in 564 B.C., Arrachion of Phigalia earned a place in the record books when his opponent, whose name is now forgotten, conceded the event because Arrachion had nearly beaten him to death. As Arrachion lay on the ground, he was declared the winner by default, but he refused to stand and claim victory. Was it because he was exhausted or perhaps overcome with the joy of victory? No. It was because he was dead. Since the bout had already been decided, Arrachion became the only dead person in history to win an Olympic event. Making the pancration less like a triathlon than a die-athlon.

THE LOSING WINNER

On October 19, 2008, New York City fifth-grade teacher Arien O'Connell ran the Nike Women's Marathon in San Francisco and posted the fastest time. She expected to be declared the winner, but she didn't even win third. The woman who did win first place, Nora Colligan, actually ran eleven minutes slower than O'Connell. So what happened? Nike had recruited a group of elite runners who were given a twenty-minute head start with the expectation that one of them would be crowned the winner. But they didn't count on O'Connell's amazing run. Colligan was declared the winner because she had a head start and she crossed the finish line first. Three days later, Nike bowed under the pressure and recognized O'Connell as the winner. Colligan and O'Connell both were awarded first place and each given a fancy bowl made by Tiffany & Company. Nike vowed that the next year it would scrap the two-tier system.

· ·

A similar situation occurred just a week before on October 12, 2008, at the Chicago Marathon, when a Kenyan named Wesley Korir finished fourth. He wasn't in the elite group and, therefore, he didn't qualify to collect fourth-place prize money even though he started five minutes after the top runners.

· ·

MORE EXCUSES, EXCUSES, EXCUSES

After falling asleep on an ice pack, left fielder Rickey Henderson missed several games in 1993 because of frostbite.

Atlanta pitcher John Smoltz suffered burns on his chest from ironing a shirt while still wearing it.

Sammy Sosa missed a game because he threw out his back when he sneezed.

Nolan Ryan was unable to pitch for Houston because of complications from a coyote bite.

Marty Cordova of the Baltimore Orioles suffered from burns to his face after spending too much time in a tanning bed.

JUST HORSING AROUND

After the fifth race at Agua Caliente Racetrack in Tijuana, Mexico, on March 13, 1934, officials had a unique dilemma on their hands. A nag called Old Kickapoo crossed the finish line first, but no one had bet any money on Old Kickapoo to win. Therefore, the track shelled out nothing on Old Kickapoo to win, but it paid a whopping $230.40 to place for every two-dollar bet. Adjusted for inflation, that would be the equivalent of nearly $4,000 in 2012 money.

• •

"There is one word in America that says it all, and that one word is, 'You never know.'"

—St. Louis Cardinals pitcher Joaquín Andújar, *Sports Illustrated*, June 22, 1987

• •

THE GREAT SPINKS

Leon Spinks was stripped of his title by the World Boxing Council for refusing to defend it against Ken Norton and agreeing instead to a return bout against Muhammad Ali. Norton is best remembered for his twelve-round victory over Muhammad Ali on March 31, 1973, in which he broke Ali's jaw. The WBC decided to award the title to Norton retroactively, designating his defeat of Jimmy Young in 1977 as a title fight. On June 9, 1978, Norton made his first defense of the title against unbeaten challenger Larry Holmes, a former sparring partner for Muhammad Ali. It was a close call, but Holmes won a split decision, with two judges favoring him 143–142 and the third giving it to Norton 144–143. Norton fought George Foreman for the World Heavyweight Championship in 1974, but was counted out after only two rounds. Making Ken Norton the only fighter in heavyweight history to be called champ without ever having won a championship fight.

. . . .

Leon Spinks is the only boxer to ever take a title belt from Muhammad Ali in the ring. But in his second fight with Ali on September 15, 1978, at the Louisiana Superdome in New Orleans, Spinks lost the title by a unanimous fifteen-round decision, making Ali the first three-time heavyweight champion.

. . . .

DROP THE BALL

The crowd was on its feet, ready for the kickoff, as Duke University's football team was preparing to take on James Madison University in Durham, North Carolina. Suddenly, two men parachuted down to the field carrying the game ball, and the crowd exploded with excitement. But there already was a ball on the field, so what's with the parachute drop? According to an August 30, 2008, article in the *Atlanta Journal-Constitution*, the two men were supposed to be delivering the game ball to a stadium ten miles away in Chapel Hill, where North Carolina was hosting McNeese State.

• •

"Jilted lesbian rugby player killed herself after brutally beating lover who had 'webcam affair'"

—*Daily Mail* headline, January 9, 2008

• •

TRADING PLACES

Trading players is nothing new in major and minor league baseball. Usually it's a trade for another player, or for money, or both. But in the case of minor league pitcher John Odom, the trade got a little batty. Odom was traded to the Calgary Vipers of the independent Golden Baseball League. But because of a 1999 aggravated assault charge, he wasn't allowed to enter Canada, so he was traded to the Laredo Broncos of the independent United League in exchange for another player. According to a May 23, 2008, Associated Press article, Odom's exchanged counterpart balked at leaving the U.S. for the Canadian team. The teams came to an agreement on May 20, 2008, to exchange Odom for ten Prairie Sticks maple bats, worth a total of $665. From that moment on, Odom was referred to by his fans as "Bat Man," "Bat Guy," or "Bat Boy."

. . . .

"His (Dwight Gooden's) reputation preceded him before he got here."

—Don Mattingly, *Sports Illustrated*, April 3, 1989

. . . .

GETTING A REAL EARFUL

Sportswriters love to turn a clever phrase in their story headlines. You have probably heard of the infamous boxing match between Mike Tyson and Evander Holyfield on June 28, 1997, commonly referred to as Holyfield–Tyson II, in which Tyson bit a chunk out of Holyfield's ear. Here are some Ear-itating headlines following that incident:

"Ear-Responsible"—*Fort Worth Star-Telegram*

"Undisputed Chomp"—*USA Today*

"From Champ to Chomp"—*Herald-Sun*, Durham, North Carolina

"Tyson's Behavior Hard to Swallow"—*Providence Journal-Bulletin*

"Sucker Munch"—*Sun*, London

"Biting Back: Evander has public's ear"—*Daily News*, New York

"It's Tyson's Nature to (Ch)eat"—*New York Post*

"Pay Per Chew"—*Philadelphia Daily News*

"Bite of the Century!"—*Arizona Republic*

"Tyson Subject of Biting Criticism"—*Baltimore Sun*

"Dracula"—*New York Post*

"Lobe Blow for Boxing"—*Tennessean*

A REAL BOOB

Alfred Rava announced that he had settled his discrimination class-action lawsuit against the Oakland A's baseball team for $500,000. According to an article in the June 18, 2009, *American Bar Association Journal*, Rava sued because he and all other men and boys in attendance at a 2004 game were denied one of 7,500 floppy hats given as a promotion for a Mother's Day breast-cancer awareness campaign. Not surprisingly, Rava, who is a lawyer, is eligible for half of the entire settlement in attorney's fees. But any other male who can prove he was one of the first 7,500 to get through the gate can claim $50.

. . . .

Milton High School beat Westlake 56–46 for the Georgia 5A boys' basketball championship, according to a March 12, 2010, account in the *Atlanta Journal-Constitution*. Westlake's chances went up in smoke during the pregame warm-ups, when Marcus Thornton, their candidate for Georgia Boys Basketball Player of the Year, sprained his ankle leaping to hip bump a teammate.

. . . .

YOU SAY POTATO AND I SAY POTA-TO

Dave Bresnahan, a catcher for the Williamsport (Pennsylvania) Bills, was behind the plate with two outs and Reading opponent Rick Lundblade on third. Bresnahan fired the ball over the head of the third baseman in what Lundblade thought was a faulty pick-off attempt. But when Lundblade trotted home, he found Bresnahan waiting for him at the plate with the ball and was tagged out. How was that possible? Sometime during the August 31, 1987, game, Bresnahan had hidden a peeled potato in his pocket, and it was the potato, not the ball, he had thrown to third. The umps ruled the runner safe and kicked Bresnahan out of the game. For what they considered "an unthinkable act," Williamsport kicked Bresnahan off the team. He left baseball in disgrace and moved to Arizona to sell real estate. But he was back the next season to take part in Williamsport's Potato Night promotion, re-create his stunt, and retire his jersey.

KICKING THE SHIN OUT OF SOMEONE

"I kind of get quite annoyed when people think that shin-kicking is quite literally two guys facing each other and kicking each other as hard as possible in the shins," said Shin-Kicking Championships judge James Wiseman. Haven't heard of the Shin-Kicking Championships? Well, they've been held on and off in Chipping Camden, England, since the 1600s. A June 6, 2012, UPI article described the event, part of the Cotswold Olimpicks, as being similar to wrestling, but in order to throw your opponent to the ground, you've got to "unbalance by kicking them first."

. . . .

In 1894, they were called the Sioux City Cornhuskers. From 1895 to 1899, they were the St. Paul Saints. From 1900 to 1903, they were the Chicago White Stockings. And from 1904 to today, they're known as the Chicago White Sox.

. . . .

LOOK BACK ON THE FUTURE

It was a long journey for the U.S. team that spent seventeen days at sea to compete in the 1896 Olympics in Athens. When they finally arrived on April 5, they believed they still had another thirteen days before the Games began to readjust and stretch their sea legs. What they didn't realize was that Greece was still using the Julian calendar. Greece did not adopt the Gregorian calendar until 1923 and, therefore, the country was twelve days ahead of most of the world. The Americans got a big surprise when they woke the next day to the announcement declaring the commencement of the games. Even with the bizarre time change, the Americans still managed to take home eleven Olympic gold medals, more than any other country.

· ·

"You can't let any team awe you. If you do, you'll wind up a horseshit player."

—Chicago White Sox shortstop Luke Appling,
The Official New York Yankees Hater's Handbook, by
William B. Mead (Putnam Publishing Group, New York, 1983)

· ·

WHAT ABOUT THE PEANUTS AND CRACKER JACK?

Everything is bigger in Texas, and now that holds true for the hot dogs, too. Sportsservice, the firm that supplies concessions at Rangers Ballpark in Arlington, Texas, announced, as reported by ESPNDallas.com on April 6, 2012, that they're introducing a one-pound hot dog. The $26 wiener was created to honor Rangers player Nelson "Boomstick" Cruz, and fittingly it's called the Boomstick. The Boomstick is topped with shredded cheese, chili, sautéed onions, and french fries. "I don't know how many calories are in this thing, but it's got to be 2,000 or 3,000," said Casey Rapp, operations manager for Sportsservice. "The bun is like a loaf of bread just to hold this thing." On Opening Day, 191 Boomsticks were served; no word on how many antacids were sold.

· ·

The Boomstick is right up there with other regional gastric delights like fried walleye (Minnesota Twins), Rocky Mountain oysters (Colorado Rockies), Ichiroll sushi (Seattle Mariners), and Crab Fries (Philadelphia Phillies).

· ·

ONE STROKE TOO FAR

At the 1983 British Open, two-time U.S. Open champ Hale Irwin was on the fourteenth green in the third round and had an easy, two-inch tap-in putt to make. He sauntered up to the ball and, with one hand, made a nonchalant one-handed swipe at the ball, missing it completely. His putter struck the ground in front of the ball and bounced over it, which counted as a stroke. "It was an unintended sword fight" with the ground, Irwin explained. One stroke can make all the difference. Because of the now infamous whiff, Irwin lost the Open to Tom Watson (his fifth Open championship) by one stroke.

"I signed with the Milwaukee Braves for three-thousand dollars. That bothered my dad at the time because he didn't have that kind of dough. But he eventually scraped it up."

—Bob Uecker, *San Francisco Examiner*, March 29, 1984

THROWN FOR A LOSS

ollowing a goal by soccer player Steve Morrow that gave Arsenal he championship in the 1993 Coca Cola Cup Final, skipper Tony .dams attempted to hoist Morrow on his shoulder for a victory elebration. The watchers' amusement at Wembley Stadium urned to shock when Adams awkwardly dropped Morrow, and he it the ground with a thud. A stretcher team came and removed Iorrow from the field, and it was soon determined that the fall ad broken his arm.

The *Charlotte Observer* reporte

on August 10, 2009, that three-

time All-American Armanti

Edwards, an Appalachian

State quarterback, was forced

to miss the first month of the

season after injuring his foot

while mowing his lawn.

A LADY'S CLUB

Margaret McNeil and Earlena Adams were tied for the lead after eighteen holes in the final round of the 1980 Boone Golf Club Championship in North Carolina, and they were forced into a sudden-death round. During her practice swing, McNeil accidentally clobbered Adams on the left forearm with her backswing and heard a snap. It wasn't her club—it was Adams's arm. Officials ruled that since Adams's arm was broken, and she could no longer play, McNeil was awarded first place by default.

· ·

The *Times* reported on October 29, 2008, that Britain's worst professional boxer, welterweight Peter Buckley, would retire after his next bout. Buckley has lost eighty-eight matches in a row; overall his record is 32–256 with twelve draws.

· ·

A PERFECT CATCH

The San Francisco Giants faced the Colorado Rockies at AT&T Park on May 28, 2006, and Giants fan Andrew Morbitzer left his bleacher seat to get beer, peanuts, and barbecue for himself and his wife. As he waited in line at the concession stand, he heard a loud roar from the crowd but had no idea what was going on. Suddenly, he saw a baseball roll off the roof, and he caught it easily with one hand. But it wasn't just any baseball—it was Barry Bonds's 715th home run (surpassing Babe Ruth's total). Morbitzer was hustled away by police so his ball could be verified as legitimate, leaving his wife in the stands wondering where her husband and her peanuts were. Several months later, Morbitzer listed the ball on eBay and accepted an offer of $220,100 for the ball. His wife, however, never did get her peanuts.

**"When I came over here
[to the National League], I
always heard it was a stronger
league, with amphetamines
all over the clubhouse, but all
I found was Michelob Dry."**

—San Francisco Giants pitcher Dan Quisenberry,
Sporting News, April 3, 1989

DISCUS CUSS

At the 1932 Olympic Summer Games in Los Angeles, California, discus thrower Jules Noël of France launched his discus farther than anyone else, but he didn't win. Why? Because the officials weren't watching. They had been distracted by the pole vault competition, and they ruled Noël's throw as unofficial. The judges allowed him another attempt, but it fell short of the first and Noël placed fourth.

· ·

In 1932, Prohibition was in effect in the United States, but the French Olympic team convinced U.S. officials that an essential part of the French diet was wine. They received special permission and, reportedly, Noël used the dispensation for all it was worth during the discus event by boozing it up with his compatriots in the locker room.

· ·

WATCH WHAT YOU WISH FOR

The famously abrasive Turkish soccer commentator Ahmet Çakar, known as Turkey's most controversial soccer pundit, is brutally critical of officials, players, fans, and even his fellow Turks. In 2004, Çakar was asked if he was afraid his strong criticism of Turkey's soccer characters would have consequences. He replied, "The worst they can do is kill me. Whoever dares can come and try and take my life. But it's not that easy . . . he who has the guts to shut me up, he who has the heart, the courage to do this, please let him come. But my flesh is thick. It's not so easy to bite." According to a February 26, 2004, Associated Press article, as he stepped out of his car in a busy area of Istanbul, Çakar was shot five times in the stomach and groin by an angry fan. True to his word, his flesh was thick, and he survived the attack.

"Ninety percent of this game is half mental."

—Yogi Berra, *Sports Illustrated*, May 14, 1979

HITTING THE HIGHEST NOTE

Actor, singer, and one of the best-selling recording artists of the twentieth century, Bing Crosby was also an avid golfer. He was informed by his doctor in 1977 that because of his declining health he should limit his golf to nine holes. Crosby took the physician's advice under consideration, but on October 14, 1977, he was golfing with a friend and two Spanish pros at La Moraleja golf course near Madrid. And what a game he was having. The crooner was leading the pack, singing, dancing, and having the time of his life, and there was no way he was going to stop at nine holes. Somewhere around the fifteenth hole, Crosby's partner noticed the seventy-four-year-old singer was favoring his left arm and asked Crosby about it. Crosby said he was fine, and the golfers finished the last three holes. It was a high note in Crosby's golf career, and he won the round, shooting an 85 for the day. Crosby shouted, "That was a great game of golf, fellas!" and promptly dropped dead.

"Gosh, all a kid has to do these days is spit straight and he gets forty thousand dollars to sign."

—Cy Young, during his speech at a tribute luncheon in Philadelphia, August 3, 1948

A UNIQUE EXCHANGE RATE

Pitcher Nigel Thatch of the Schaumburg Flyers of the Northern League, a professional baseball league in the northern United States and Canada, was traded on May 1, 2006. According to the official league announcement, the Flyers "assigned the contract of RHP Nigel Thatch (Rookie) to Fullerton of the Golden Baseball League in exchange for one pallet (60 cases) of Budweiser beer." In a case of life imitating art, Thatch portrayed the character of Leon in several Budweiser commercials.

WHILE IN ZIMBABWE FOR A SOCCER MATCH, THE SIXTEEN MEMBERS OF A TEAM CALLED MIDLAND PORTLAND CEMENT WERE TOLD THAT A CEREMONIAL SWIM IN THE ZAMBEZI RIVER WOULD CLEANSE THE TEAM OF EVIL SPIRITS. ACCORDING TO AN OCTOBER 7, 2008, REUTERS ARTICLE, THERE WAS NO REPORT ABOUT ANY EVIL SPIRITS BEING SUCCESSFULLY REMOVED, BUT THE SWIM DID PERMANENTLY REMOVE ONE OF THE TEAM'S PLAYERS SINCE THERE ARE CROCODILES IN THE ZAMBEZI.

GETTING TEED OFF

Jeannine Pelletier had played golf at the Fort Kent Golf Club in Maine about twenty times before her accident on September 6, 1995. She teed off at the first hole of the little nine-hole golf course, and her ball landed about fourteen yards from a set of old railroad tracks. She eyed the green and took a mighty swing at the ball, which shot out like a rocket, hit the railroad tracks, ricocheted back, and hit Pelletier directly on the nose. Pelletier sued the golf course for negligence, seeking $250,000 in damages. The jury didn't completely believe Pelletier's golf story and found that she was partially to blame for the accident herself. The jury awarded Pelletier only $40,000. Harold J. Friedman, the Portland attorney whose law firm represented the golf course, explained that a golfer who struck a tree or a rock could have suffered the same injury. "This case doesn't belong in the courts," Friedman said. "The plaintiff should have seen her golf pro to straighten out her swing." The award was appealed, but the Supreme Judicial Court of Maine agreed with the trial court and, in July 1994, let Pelletier keep the $40,000 award. At the same time, however, it denied Pelletier's husband the damages he had sought. Gerard Pelletier was suing for damages because Mrs. Pelletier's nose was so sore she wouldn't allow him to have sex with her. "On the evidence before it," the Supreme Judicial Court stated, "the jury properly could have concluded that as a result of the injuries sustained by his wife, Gerard suffered no loss of continuation of relationship with her." Looks like Jeannine landed in the green and Gerard landed in the rough.

NOW, GO OUT THERE AND LOSE ONE FOR THE GIPPER

"I used to try to give them a pep talk . . . but I found out I was just making them nervous," said coach Joseph Fink of the Friendsville Academy Foxes (Tennessee). "One boy started shaking and dropped a cup of water all over the place." The Foxes accrued 138 losses in a row between 1967 and 1973, a stunningly pitiful record unequaled in high school basketball history. In 1970, Phil Patterson was named as Friendsville's outstanding player even though he had not scored a single point. In an interview with Douglas S. Looney from the *National Observer*, Fink expressed his coaching style and opinion of his team:

> **Looney:** Is there anything this team does well?
> **Coach:** Not really.
> **Looney:** Are you making any progress?
> **Coach:** I couldn't truthfully say that we are.
> **Looney:** Do you like coaching?
> **Coach:** I don't care that much for basketball.

During the next season, Rick Little coached the team, and the Foxes losing streak finally came to an end when they beat St. Camillus Academy of Corbin, Kentucky, which had lost forty-eight in a row. Contemplating his victory streak of one, the team's new coach said, "Oh well, you can't lose them all."

FASTEST WAY OUT

Daredevil Donald Campbell broke eight world speed records in the 1950s and 1960s and remains the only person to set both the world land speed record (403.10 miles per hour) and water speed record (276.33 miles per hour) in the same year (1964). But on January 4, 1967, Campbell set out to blow the speed record out of the water by attempting to travel more than 300 miles per hour on water. He fired up his jet-engine powerboat *Bluebird K7* on Coniston Water, a lake in England, and pushed it to an amazing 310 miles per hour—but at a price. When the *Bluebird* reached a peak speed of 320 miles per hour, it started bouncing furiously. Campbell's last words via radio were, "I can't see much and the water's very bad indeed . . . I can't get over the top . . . I'm getting a lot of bloody row in here . . . I can't see anything . . . I've got the bows out . . . I'm going! . . . (grunt)." Donald Campbell's body and his boat were lost under the water.

. . . .

The *Bluebird* Project was established to raise Campbell's wrecked boat. In October 2000, the first sections of the *Bluebird* were raised, and in June 2001 divers were able to finally recover Campbell's body.

. . . .

FINAL NAME GAME TEAM ROSTER

Baseball Teams from the International League (1884–Present)

1895, SPRINGFIELD MAROONS

1896–1900, SPRINGFIELD PONIES

1894, TROY WASHER WOMEN

1885–1887, UTICA PENTUPS

1899–1900, WORCESTER FARMERS

. . . .

The Bloomington, Indiana, *Herald-Times* reported on October 12, 2000, that a thirty-year-old man was shot to death at a bar in Spencer, Indiana, by a fan of race car driver Dale Earnhardt. The Earnhardt fan was outraged that the victim was wearing a Jeff Gordon cap.

. . . .

THE KING'S DECREE

"Forasmuch as there is great noise in the city caused by the hustling over large balls from which many evils might arise which God forbid; we commend and forbid, on behalf of the King, on pain of imprisonment, such game to be used in the city in the future."

—King Edward II of England, April 13, 1314, banning the game of soccer

"**He [Branch Rickey] must think
I went to the Massachusetts
Constitution of Technology.**"

—St. Louis Cardinals pitcher Dizzy Dean
Sporting News, March 26, 193

STILL MORE EXCUSES, EXCUSES, EXCUSES

Atlanta outfielder Terry Harper separated his shoulder after high-fiving a teammate.

Chicago Cubs pitcher Carlos Zambrano was put on the disabled list after being diagnosed with carpal tunnel syndrome, a result of spending too much time on the Internet.

Minnesota pitcher Terry Mulholland was forced to sit out several games after he scratched his eye on a feather sticking out of a pillow.

When he tried to open a DVD case with a knife, San Diego pitcher Adam Eaton accidentally stabbed himself.

THAT'S HOW THEY ROLL

Scott Browning of Houston, Texas, was awarded $16,500 in damages in 1996 from the Men's Club in Houston. Browning ruptured his Achilles tendon during a club-sponsored golf tournament when an exotic dancer, assigned to be his designated caddie and cart driver, became so drunk she overturned their cart into a drainage canal.

• •

From the column "This Week's Sign That The Apocalypse Is Upon Us," *Sports Illustrated* **reported on July 24, 1995, that Texas Rangers relief pitcher Ed Vosberg received a citation outside the Rangers Ballpark in Arlington for illegally trying to scalp four complimentary tickets to the All-Star Game.**

• •

WHAT, NO TOILET BOWL?

On January 1, 1948, five new college bowl games debuted. Ole Miss won over TCU 13–9 in the Delta Bowl (Memphis). Arkansas barely edged out a 21–19 victory over William and Mary in the Dixie Bowl (Birmingham). Hardin–Simmons slaughtered San Diego State 53–0 in the Harbor Bowl (San Diego). Pacific trounced Wichita 26–14 in the Raisin Bowl (Fresno, California). Nevada–Reno chopped up North Texas 13–9 in the Salad Bowl (Phoenix). The Delta, Dixie, and Harbor Bowls died in '49, and the Raisin and Salad Bowls were history by 1951.

. . . .

Appearing on HBO's *Real Sports with Bryant Gumbel*, and reported in the *Sunday Gazette* (October 21, 1995), Dallas Cowboys owner Jerry Jones said, "There's no ego in my life. But fifteen, twenty years ago, I was wandering around Arkansas, and Bill Clinton was running around Arkansas. Who would have ever thought that one would go on to power, prestige, and fame. And the other one end up as president of the United States."

. . . .

NO STOMACH FOR THE GAME

David Robinson graduated from the Naval Academy in 1987, and was selected by the San Antonio Spurs in the NBA Draft, but he was unable to play for two years because he had to fulfill his active-duty obligation with the navy. So on November 4, 1989, everyone was anxious for the debut of "The Admiral" (so called because he was considered to be the best basketball player in U.S. Naval Academy history) when he appeared on the boards to face the Los Angeles Lakers. The HemisFair Arena in Alamo City was packed with excited fans who watched as, early in the game, Robinson tossed one out. He didn't toss the ball—he tossed his cookies. In other words, Robinson threw up on the court. Later, reporters asked if his upchucking was simply a case of nerves, but Robinson tried to convince them the cause was a bad fajita he'd eaten in Milwaukee—a week earlier.

RUNNING ABREAST

Talk about playing out of the rough. While playing in the RBC Heritage golf classic at Hilton Head Island, South Carolina, tourney leader Hale Irwin's tee shot careened into the crowd and clonked a female spectator. The woman was not hurt, but she had an extra lump on her chest—the ball had become lodged down her blouse. PGA officials huddled and ruled the November 28, 1971, miss-tee an unplayable lie (not sure if the woman appreciated the ruling, however). Irwin was allowed a free drop, and he went on to take first place.

In a photo accompanying a story about a disc injury suffered by Dallas Cowboys cornerback Deion Sanders, the caption in the August 17, 1997, issue of the Greenville, Texas, *Herald Banner* said that Sanders "does not expect a bulging dick in his back to slow him down on the football field."

BEAN COUNTER

Andy Bean was on the fifteenth green during the third round at the 1983 Canadian Open when his ball came to rest a mere two inches from the cup. In an attempt at ill-conceived showmanship, Bean spun his putter upside down and tapped the ball into the cup using the grip. The smile on his face quickly disappeared when he remembered Rule 14-1, which states, "The ball shall be fairly struck at with the head of the club and must not be pushed, scraped or spooned." Bean was assessed a two-stroke penalty. The next day, he shot a 62 in the final round but missed the playoff—by two strokes.

. . . .

"My job isn't to strike guys out, it's to get them out, sometimes by striking them out."

—New York Mets pitcher Tom Seaver,
New York Times, January 11, 1976

. . . .

A SHOE STORY

Adolf "Adi" Dassler and his older brother Rudolf were the sons of a poor shoe-factory worker and his laundress wife from the tiny Bavarian town of Herzogenaurach, near Nuremburg. Before World War II, they started a factory there called *Gebrüder Dassler Schuhfabrik* (Dassler Brothers Shoe Factory). But after the war, the two brothers had a violent falling-out and went their separate ways. Adolf started producing track and soccer shoes in his new company, called Adidas, from his nickname "Adi" and the first three letters of his last name, and not as an acronym for All Day I Dream About Sport. His brother started a competing sports shoe company, called Puma. Before long, Adidas and Puma—both headquartered in Herzogenaurach—were battling head-to-head all over the world. When Rudolph died in 1974, the two brothers hadn't spoken to each other in twenty-five years.

. . . .

"When I came up to bat with three men on and two outs in the ninth, I looked in the other team's dugout, and they were already in street clothes."

—Bob Uecker, *Baseball Digest*, June 1972

. . . .

THE BOTTOMLEY OF THE BARREL

Like a lot of politicians, Horatio Bottomley was not only an ex-member of the English Parliament, but he was also a convicted fraud artist. Bottomley devised what he thought was an ingenious and foolproof plan to scam some big money on the ponies. In 1914, he deduced that if he bought all six horses in the race, hired his own jockeys, and told them in which order he wanted them to finish, he could clean up. So he did just that. Bottomley must have been rubbing his hands together in anticipation of a huge payday when something happened that he hadn't anticipated—fog. A thick pea-soup fog poured in over the track during the middle of the race. It was so dense the jockeys couldn't see each other, and they had no idea in which order they were running. When the announcer called out the order, Bottomley had lost every bet he placed.

· ·

"It would depend how well she (his mother) was hitting (in answer to whether he would throw at his mom also)."

—Cleveland Indians pitcher Early "Gus" Wynn,
Baseball Digest, April 1970

· ·

FOR THE GLOVE OF THE GAME

For a fan, there's no greater thrill than catching a ball during a major league game. In fact, dozens of fans bring their gloves, just in case. But in 1922, the rules were a little different, as eleven-year-old Robert Cotter found out. He was attending a Philadelphia Phillies game when one of the players hit a foul ball into the stands, and Cotter managed to grab it. Of course, he wanted to keep it, but in the early days, baseballs were too expensive for teams to allow such a practice. Fans were expected to simply toss the balls back onto the field, but young Cotter refused, even when security guards ordered him to give the ball back. So what did they do to the young lad? They took him to jail. Cotter spent the night in jail for refusing to give back the ball. The next morning, he appeared in front of a judge, who ordered that he be set free. "Such an act on the part of a boy is merely proof that he is following his most natural impulses," the disgusted judge said. "It is a thing I would do myself." Unfortunately, Cotter never did get his ball back, but that summer, a woman in New York read about what the boy had been through and invited him to New York to watch the Yankees play the Philadelphia Athletics. She arranged for Cotter to get an autographed baseball that he could keep, and he even got to meet Babe Ruth.

A HARD ROW TO HOE

Soviet Vyacheslav Ivanov, one of the most accomplished rowers of his generation, was in second place with two-hundred meters remaining in the two-thousand-meter single sculls at the 1956 Olympics in Melbourne, Australia. He quickly overtook Australian Stuart MacKenzie, who had stopped rowing because he believed he had won the race, and captured the gold with a time of eight minutes, two and a half seconds. At the medals ceremony, Ivanov was so excited he accidentally dropped his gold medal into Lake Wendouree, where the rowing events were held. He dove into the lake in a vain attempt to recapture the gold, but he failed, and the medal was lost forever. However, the International Olympic Committee provided him with a replacement.

• •

Teams soon realized that they couldn't imprison everyone who kept a ball, so they acquiesced and allowed fans to keep game balls. An interviewer from *USA Today* asked Cotter in 1998 if he felt responsible for baseball's change of heart. "I'm not sure if I caused that," he said. "I was only eleven."

• •

"There are two theories on hitting the knuckleball. Unfortunately, neither one of them works."

—Charlie Lau, *The 1989 Baseball Card Engagement Book*,
by Michael Gershman (Houghton Mifflin, Boston, 1989)